To John
- A Kindred Soul
Love



# My Search for the Infinite

***My twelve years as a private student of Joel S. Goldsmith***

**Evelyn Brill Stark**

*with*

*Dr. Sven-Erik Ljungholm*

***Chester Publishing***

**Chester, Ct. USA**



Cover design and artwork by Gary Perrett

Back cover photo by: Robert Booth

CHESTER PUBLISHING

**www.mysearchfortheinfinite.com**

*Every effort has been made to secure necessary permission to use copyrighted materials. In the event of any questions arising as to their use, the publisher will immediately make any necessary changes in future printings.*

**ISBN 0-9724636-0-7**
**$16.95**

ISBN 0-9724636-0-7

51695

9 780972 463607

Other books by Evelyn Brill Stark include LIFE IS A POEM, *Often Set to Music,* Southfarm Press P.O. Box 1296, Middletown, Ct. 06457

"God is ever before my eyes. I realize His omnipotence and I fear His anger; but I also recognize His love, His compassion, and His tenderness toward all His creatures"

*Wolfgang Amadeus Mozart*

# Foreword

***When I was a child, I talked like a child, felt like a child, reasoned like a child:***
***When I became mature, I put from me childish ways.***

**1 Corinthians 13:11 St. Paul**

St. Paul wrote, and it has been said time and again, that there is nothing new under the sun. You have every reason then to ask, why am I writing about something that has been spoken and written about more than any other subject since the beginning of time. Well, for me it is for perfectly valid reasons.

Through these words I wish to express again my gratitude to God for His loving, consistent and compelling *search* for me… as I sought for Him. I would also like to share how that search helped form my spirituality through these 88 years of living in that experience. I hope and pray that these words may help someone else who is searching, help make their search richer, fuller and less exhausting. For others I know my story will be a reaffirmation of what they already know and believe, thereby making the foundation of their faith ever more unyielding.

I do not think my childhood faith or search for a spiritual love was really much different from most of you reading this introduction. How that search developed, however, is unique. I sensed early on, when just four or five-years-old, an innermost, intuitive search for love. I was born and raised in New York City and never wanted for anything material. Every possible comfort was provided me. But what I sensed lacking in my life, especially at home, was love. Perhaps that is why my search began so early. God revealed Himself to me many times in my youth and early adulthood. However, my unconscious was never fully content. I did not sense fulfillment. None-the-less, for more than 40 years, God opened Himself to me by coming to my rescue many times, and by doing so reminded me of His absolute presence and power.

In my early adulthood, my unconscious continued to unfold and I turned to the Eastern religions. I concentrated all my energies on seeking the Truth. Among the teachers were Lao-tzu, Ramakrishna, Aurobindo, Krishnamurti. A yogi I met, Ralph Houston, inspired my study of the Eastern religions.

My thirst for a deeper understanding of God continued. He led me to a spiritual teacher, one with whom I eventually established a very close relationship. God led me to Joel Goldsmith, author of *The Infinite Way.*

I read, studied and meditated on all that Joel had written. For years, he gave classes all over the world. As soon as audiotapes of his lectures became available I sent for them. For eight years I listened alone in my den to the tapes that arrived from Hawaii, where he lived. I listened to them over and over again until they became a part of my consciousness.

After eight years of listening, studying and meditating on his words, I wrote Joel and asked if he would accept me as a private student. I was privileged to learn at the feet of the author in both public and private visits, from California to Chicago to New York. St. Paul wrote, "You must die to your former self." I converted to not only a new philosophy, but to a doctrine that helped me understand that conversion meant moving from death to life.

Joel's message became my message, and I worked tirelessly for many years distributing his books and audio recordings throughout the world. I recorded an audiocassette wherein I shared my violin playing, my poetry and my writings. God had blessed me with a love and a gift for writing. I was first published at age 14, and recently I learned that a three-part article I wrote, at 88-years-of age, would be published in England in 2002. To think that I have been privileged to carry the ageless message from one century into another; to think that Joel Goldsmith inspired me to be God's messenger!

The message?

It is very simple. When you understand the nature of God as all Power, all Wisdom, and all Presence, and you know with complete certainty that nothing exists but God, then you realize that whenever you love anything or anyone you are really loving God. It means that God, the one and only presence, is manifesting Himself as all of creation, that His consciousness is the consciousness of everyone and everything that exists. And since His consciousness is spiritual, everything that exists must be spiritual. It means that His consciousness is your consciousness, your own individual consciousness. And since His consciousness is infinite, then your consciousness must be infinite too.

My book is the story of my journey, and you who are seeking the things of the Spirit are invited to join in this adventure. If at the end of the journey you feel something inside of you that was not there before, a new awareness perhaps, a heightened realization of the beautiful simplicity of life as it was meant to be lived, you will know you were meant to come along.

*Evelyn Brill Stark* Chester, Ct. 2002

# Chapter 1

## THE SEARCH FOR THE INFINITE

### The Search

**"To whom do we belong?**
**This is the core question of the spiritual life.**

**Do we belong to the world, its worries,**
**its people and its endless chain of urgencies and emergencies,**
**or do we belong to God and God's people? "**

Henri Nouwen, *Behold the Beauty of the Lord*

Thomas Merton wrote, "At the center of our being is a point of nothingness which is untouched by sin and by illusion, a point of pure truth, a point or spark which *belongs* entirely to God...." God establishes His presence in the life of every person by touching the soul, the home of His spirit in us. From birth, when He deems it timely, God will step into each life to remind us of the awesomeness of His creation, His majestic presence and His planned relationship with us.

God seeks and expects a response. He waits and longs for each person to move toward seeking His spirit and His unique purpose and plan for each life. Meister Eckhart tells us, "The seed of God is in us. Given an intelligent and hard-working farmer, it will thrive and grow up to God, whose seed it is; and accordingly its fruits will be God-nature. Pear seeds grow into pear trees, nut seeds into nut trees, and God-seed into God."

The possibility and realization of experiencing our *belonging* to God is innate. "I found Thee not, O Lord, without, because I erred in seeking Thee without that wert within.." wrote St. Augustine

Most religious persons, those with a spiritual experience of belonging to the Eternal, can identify and detail when and how they came to a realization that they were part of something greater than themselves. Many will point to a family member, or family tradition. Others testify to a person in their religious community as being significant in bringing about their religious or conversion experience. Some will share that their enlightenment came about through reading spiritually provoking texts. And some will share that nature or other significant phenomena illumined their soul. All seeking persons though, I believe, would speak of a motivation requiring connecting to, and being rooted in God.

My own experience was the latter. Although born in a Jewish home, and with family, friends and other persons around me with strong religious roots, my search for belonging was private and innate. I knew early in life that I lacked nothing, at least in the material sense of the word. Everything I could possibly want to make life comfortable was provided me. However, my need for belonging to the Eternal could not be quenched by outside sources, pat answers or being smothered by the material in life.

No modern theologian in my mind has probed the human passion "to belong" more deeply than Simone Weil. A confirmed agnostic early in life (1909-1943). born a secular French Jewess in a comfortable setting, she graduated from the prestigious Ecole Normale Academy. She led an ascetic existence long before the mystical experience in which Christ took possession of her.

In the last book she wrote, *The Need for Roots*, she reflects positively on the importance of religious and political social structures in the life of the individual. For Weil, the contingency of human existence required human beings to fulfill their religious "image" through belonging to the Creator.

Nouwen's *To Whom Do We Belong*?, posed many of the same questions that I had raised. My search for roots mirrored Weil's. To understand the spiritual tension fully, I need to bring you back to my earliest recollections of my encounter with God as a child, and subsequently, how I sought God as an adult.

I remember as a child, at a youth camp in Maine, lying on my back on a clear night gazing at a sky emblazoned with stars. My mind was aghast at the massiveness of the heavenly bodies, God's creation, my universe. And as I sought to take it all in, there began a natural and earnest search for my soul to penetrate beyond the universe that my eyes could see, to what my *heart* might see. I sought to reach into the very heart of God, the Creator, beyond the fathomless immensity above me. The wonder of His creation convinced an eight-year-old girl of His awesomeness, and that He would respond to my search.

No doubt the shepherd David stretched out in a similar fashion, while tending sheep on a Judean hillside 3,000 years earlier when he wrote: *"O LORD, our Lord, how majestic is your name in all the earth! You have set your glory above the heavens. From the lips of children and infants you have ordained praise..."* Although I wasn't familiar with the Psalms, truly the thoughts that fluttered in and out of my mind echoed the songs of David.

David's words reflect the plea and praise of each gazing soul longing to see beyond the skies. His psalm mirrors the spiritual yearning of every man. He evokes the full range of human emotions, from fear and despair, to courage and admiration, from complaint and frustration, to praise and thanksgiving.

**The Answer**

**THE PERFECT SOLUTION**

**"Hell hath no fury like a woman scorned"**
**And for my lost loves in deep pain I have mourned**
**My eyes are now open to truths of my past**
**My heart which was broken understands why at last**
**The love I was seeking was not to be found**
**In the human attachments to which I was bound**

**Illusion, delusion had caused such confusion**
**It forced me to go into inner seclusion**
**Reflection, selection led to a direction**
**Transcending all ties of an earthly connection.**

**Revealing the feelings of Love's sweet perfection**
**The Joy and the Peace of Eternal protection**
**My heart has been cleansed by this inner ablution**
**Letting God (grace- love) live my life is the perfect solution**

Evelyn Brill Stark

"Thy grace is my sufficiency" I live by Thy grace.

I recall how God answered me again and again, and where. He next lit a flame in the *heart* of an eleven-year-old girl, at a sleep away camp several hundred miles from her Manhattan home. I know that it was not my imagination when He sent those stars, flitting this way and that through the star-studded sky. It was as though God was winking at me – flirting with me! I am reminded of the words of A.W. Tozer, "An infinite God can give all of Himself to each of His children. He does not distribute Himself that each may have a part, but to each one He gives all of Himself as fully as if there were no others." That is how it felt those many years ago... It was as though it was only God and I that existed!

I was very young when I had that first mystical communion with God. It was my nature seeking God, who is love. I felt as though God had created the universe just for me, for me to admire, reflect on, and strive toward His love, His glory. Through His created universe He demonstrated His love for me. And in several successive years I returned to that same hillside spot to commune with Him.

Thinking back now, some 75 years later about that camp in Maine, I understand fully why it became such a special place for me, and why I had to return to it each summer. It was the place where I took my first steps in knowing to Whom I belong.

**My Faith – His Response**

I'm eight-years-old and I'm in Barker, Maine, with my parents and sister Adele. She is ten months and ten days older than I am.

Adele and I are in the office of the Barker Hotel and Cottages, a small private resort. We are reading a poster on the bulletin board announcing a "Junior Tennis Tournament" for our age group at the resort. There would be a trophy medal for the winner. Even though we knew very little about how to play tennis, my sister and I signed up. Even if we lost out in the first round it would be more fun than not being in the tournament at all.

All I could think of for the next three weeks was the tennis tournament. It was impossible but – what if I were to win? What would the children think? What would Daddy and Mother think? I began talking to God. *"Are you for real? If you do exist could you help me with the tennis tournament? Could you help me win it?"*

My governess had given me a present of some tiny cherubs. I hung them in the window and spoke to them every night. I asked God through them to help me win the tournament. Every night in bed I sent up questions to God. Could He do anything? I never stopped. Night after night I talked to God about the tennis tournament. The day of the tournament finally arrived.

Don't ask me how, but somehow I made it to the finals where I was to compete with the boy everyone knew was going to win. Even before the tournament, people were talking about how he was sure to win because he was by far the best junior player in the colony and no one could even come near him. But I wasn't giving up on it. God had done a wonderful job for me so far, and I wasn't going to give up now.

The day arrived for the finals and there I was, standing on the tennis court, ready for whatever would happen. The ball came and I hit it. It came again. I hit it again. It came again and again and again and I hit it as hard as I could. Always the ball landed in the right place. Only it wasn't I who was hitting it. Something or someone was moving my arm and all I did was go along with it. And then I heard the words, and they couldn't have been clearer; "*God helps those who help themselves*."

I still have the medal, and it represents more than winning the tournament. It is God's reply to my question. "Are you for real?"

The next few years were full of adventure. School was going well as were my music studies. My life was full and I forgot about God.

A few years later, however, I again sought God's help, this time in a more meaningful and serious pursuit than the tennis tournament. I was the valedictorian of my high school graduation class at the DeLancey School for Girls in New York, at age 15, and my heart was set on going to Barnard College (Columbia University). It meant everything to me. But, there was a big problem. At that time Barnard had a quota of accepting only 20 percent of its Jewish applicants – and I was Jewish.

My main obstacles were the College Board entrance exams in math and geography. One third of the math exam would contain a kind of problem in which there was a blank area in my brain. The geography exam entailed knowing maps of remote areas of the world, which was simply too much for me to study. But my desire to get into Barnard was so strong that, for months before the College Boards came up, I tried "to make a deal" with God. Every night when I went to bed I pleaded with God with my whole being. "Please *get me into Barnard. If you get me into Barnard, I'll have faith in you.*" It was a similar plea I had made years earlier in Maine. Maybe it shouldn't even be called a prayer, but it couldn't have been more intense and it was the only way I knew of talking to God. As it turned out later, He must have heard me.

A week before I was to take the College Boards I fell and hurt my knee so badly I was confined to bed. The day of the exam I was in so much pain that I needed the help of two men to help me into a taxi and take me to the testing center at Barnard College. When the test began, everyone was handed a little blue exam book. I looked mine over and sure enough, there was the one-area on math that I could not cope with. I left it blank and did my best to make the other two-thirds perfect. Because the other students were working on all three areas, I finished my exam before they did and tried to get up to hand in my blue book. But the pain in my leg became so intense I could not raise myself from the chair. As I sat there, I glanced down at the book and the miracle happened. The answers to every blank space were given to me. I wrote them down, checked and double-checked them, and I knew they were correct. I knew I was handing in a near-perfect exam.

*Who gave me the answers?*

The geography exam came next. Again, due to my injury, I required the assistance of two men to help me to the test center. The night before the exam I decided to take my chances on the maps; it would be impossible to learn all of them. As the taxi made its way to Barnard College, I started shuffling the pages in the map book when, to my surprise, one page in the book remained open. I glanced down at the map on that page and memorized as much of it as I could. That was the map featured on the exam! I was ready.

*Who opened that page for me?*

My summer months were again spent in Maine and a telegram was delivered to camp, from mother. It read: "Tell Evelyn she has been admitted to Barnard". Our whole graduating class had taken the College Boards exams and I found out later I was the only one who had been accepted.

*God had not only heard my prayer, He answered it!*

**Connecting - Rooting**

Years went by and I forgot about God. All I cared about was boys and having fun.

In my initial search for God on that hillside, and subsequently, through winning the tennis tournament and getting into Barnard, my faith had been validated. But it was a belief in a *faith* rather than a belief in the *object* of that -- God. I did not realize then what I now know. God rewards each search by allowing the seeker to "connect" with His spirit. We must come to Him in a childlike submission, in humility, without pride. When I sought His spirit past the stars of those summer evenings in Maine, He revealed Himself to the seeking child that I was, and my soul was filled in a wondrous way.

I realized early in life, and the realization was substantiated time and again, that in order for me to sense any semblance of fullness, my soul had to feel connected with the Eternal. God created me spiritually in His image. He is the Father and I am the child. And in the very same way as the prodigal's heart yearned for home, my heart did too. The prodigal turned homeward. And I did too.

**Home**

**There is no rest for me**
**Until I am home in Thee**
**So softly I pray, and follow the Way**
**Although we've seemed far apart**
**I know that within my heart**
**Your love guides me homeward**
**Your love guides me home**

Evelyn Brill Stark

Although I matured intellectually, my spiritual maturity was not keeping step. I began to sense that God was seeking me to give more of my spirit and will over to Him. When I was a child I felt God was there for my purposes. Now, I sensed that He was seeking me for His purposes. I sensed His presence, but it was mostly on my terms. I began to realize that God must possess me before I can have a sense of His constant presence with me.

I was 25 years old when I realized that it was as if the depth of my inner being was rebelling against the superficial way I was living and behaving in the world I had been raised. The depth of my subconscious demanded to be heard. It became unmistakably clear to me that I had to explore and discover a meaning in life beyond my limited environment. Instinctively, I felt there must be more to life than the way I was living it with my family and friends. Questions kept coming up. Who am I? What is this life all about? To whom do I belong? In this mysterious, beautiful, crazy, unfathomable world, what is most worth striving for?

As I pondered these questions, quite suddenly, they merged and took form in one gigantic question. And it would not let me rest until I gave it a satisfactory answer. Apparently it was not only a perplexing question for my mind alone, because a popular contemporary book of that day by Paul Tillich quickly became a classic, *Dynamics of Faith.* The book's instant popularity stemmed from its study of man's ultimate concern, my concern, a concern that remains the same from age to age. The question was quite simply: "What is the Greatest (Most Important) Thing in the World?"

It was then the idea was born. I would conduct a survey on the subject, "What is the Greatest Thing in the World?" I sent letters to people in all walks of life – successful and some not so successful, writers, teachers, doctors, businessmen, anyone and everyone who had something to say.

The response was immediate and enthusiastic. The answers were as varied as were the respondents. Money and power had their champions as well as character and humility. But there was one answer that far outnumbered the others, mother love.

After reading and rereading the letters there was one theme that became prominent. Will Durant's words were quoted in one of the letters, as though speaking for the lot:

Motherhood is the highest symbol of that creative force which hides behind mechanism. Her sole equal is the genius, the vehicle of spiritual creation, the maker of new knowledge and new values. In motherhood and genius – there above all is God. Reverence for mothers and children and all growing things, loyalty to life… this is the worship of God.

No matter the number of responses nor the number settling on the same reply, I soon realized the magnitude of my delusion in ever having believed that the ideals and lofty thoughts of others could ever deter or dull my soul's need for a personal answer. The search was mine and mine alone. No looking outside to others for what they might think. The answer for me, if there was any, had to be found within myself, and if it were to mean anything it would have to be proven by being lived.

When I realized this, the real search began and I entered a new life. The substance and sustenance of my new life was love. The nature of it was in complete accord with my deepest longings and it ended in fulfillment. It was love between a man and a woman that embodied passion, tenderness, protectiveness, appreciation, respect, understanding, sympathy, and depth.

Deeper and beyond that I discovered another kind of love which transcends this…. my affinity for the spiritual, which includes faith and trust and hope for tomorrow.

Today, seven decades later, my life experience relates closely with Simone Weil. “To be rooted,” wrote Weil, “is perhaps the most important and least recognized need of the human soul.” For Weil, “rooted” meant denying one’s ego and status in society. In a similar sense, I began seeking to be rooted in God, becoming a member of His family, and in the depth of my humility I sought Him and His spirit filled my spirit.

God delights in reminding, assuring, and demonstrating His love by allowing us to be rooted in Him. And in demonstrating His love, He makes us feel that our spirit is one with His. I didn’t know this as a child, how *His spirit sought mine, now I do*, and my heart is overflowing with love and gratitude because it knows so deeply and so surely that the Father and I are one. I belong to Him.

**Fulfillment**

**Be still and know, Be still and know that I am God**
**Be still and know that I will never leave you child**
**Be still and know that I and thee are one**

**For thou art mine and I am thine**
**Forever more to be - at one with Me -**
**For I and thee and thee in me eternally**
**Beloved child through all eternity**

**So let it be and rest in me**
**Before thy call I will answer whatever thy need**
**Closer than breathing My presence in thee**
**Knowing thy thoughts and thy fears**

**Give all to Me, thy heart thy soul, thy mind**
**Give thyself up in surrender to Me**
**Give thyself up to my love**
**Be still and know, Be still and know,**
**Know I will never leave you child**
**Be still and know my Love**

Evelyn Brill Stark

# Chapter 2

### Encounters with the INFINITE

**Life is not measured by the number of breaths we take, but by the moments that take our breath away**

The Infinite broke into my reality throughout my childhood, teen years and again in my early twenties. It broke into my moments of need and His presence took my breath away. My life though was far from serendipitous. The visits of the Infinite were sporadic coming only at those times when I called out for help, seeking an assurance of love. Life by its very nature will bring with it tragedy but one doesn't expect to find it at home or have it reinforced throughout childhood.

My mother often said that my sister Adele "had been given beauty, and you Evelyn, were graced with intellect." Even though the word "grace" was thrown in, I never perceived it as a loving sentiment.

Father died and went to heaven when I was 14. Being a spiritual and godly man, I was sure that he had earned this reward. But after he died I really had no one to talk to about my anxiety, my feeling of inadequacy that mother would so often reinforce. Her comments struck at the center of my self-esteem and stunted my emotional growth. I felt like Cinderella. Fortunately though, our family at home included Selma, our governess. She came to live with us when I was five years old. She was the only person in my home, after my father's death, from whom I sensed any love. During the years that Selma lived in our home, I turned to her for the affection that I so desperately sought from mother.

I loved Selma and she loved me. I penned this poem about Selma at the time I wrote my first book, *Life Is A Poem*,

**Selma**

**How she always was there**
**To answer my need.**
**How she poured out her love**
**When my heart had to bleed.**
**How she nurtured the soil**
**Of my potential seed.**
**Yes Selma, my Selma,**
**You blessed me indeed.**

Selma was my dearest friend and constant companion during my formative years. When mother took my sister and me shopping or on excursions Selma was always along. As soon as we arrived at a store, mother and Adele would disappear, off on their own without a word to Selma and me. When we went on excursions it was the same – they disappeared to this place or that. Selma and I would make no attempt to join them, knowing that our company was not wanted.

I had lost any honest joy in my soul as a child. Since mother made no effort to bring even a modicum of comfort I tried often to make amends with her but to no avail. My pleadings were met more than once with derisive laughter. I felt abandoned and Selma no doubt sensed this and did her best to make up for it. Selma was both my friend and surrogate mother.

I loved Selma and always sought to find a way to please her. One of my proudest moments was when I surprised her, at age 8, by reciting David's $23^{rd}$ Psalm. Selma had read it to me many times, and each time I pictured myself tending sheep. I saw how the flock would follow me through a barren countryside. They followed me because they knew that I would lead them until I found just the right pasture, rich in foliage with a brook nearby where the sheep could lap up the cool running waters. I would watch the lambs romp and play in the shade of giant trees. Sometimes a young lamb would trip and fall. Bleating, it would rush to me knowing that I would lift it into my lap, caress and soothe it. Then, once comforted and reassured of my love it would dash off again to join its friends. That Psalm has remained my favorite for 80 years- *Thou leadeth me beside the still waters - Thy rod and Thy staff they comfort me – Thou restoreth my soul.*

Selma sought to teach me early in life that my comfort was to be found "within". She instilled the knowledge that the Shepherd was seeking me. I was one of His lambs. As she read me Bible stories the emptiness within faded. A wonderful serene sense of joy and peace filled me. In those moments my unconscious began a search for God that, although answered sporadically, comforted the soul of a young Manhattan girl through her teens, high school years and into college.

My college days were wonderful. I was a top student and my social calendar was full of excitement. There was also my music, my violin, which I studied for years with great joy. My life long love for poetry remained rewarded as many of the poems I wrote were recognized and published. It was during this flurry of activity that I met Morty, my husband to be. Our introduction to each other came at the instigation of my mother and her best friend. Looking back on those years it now seems like my life at that time was almost programmed.

I met Morty on a blind date the year I graduated from college. A year later, in 1933, we were married. Both of us knew intuitively from the moment we met that we were meant to be together, and so we were wed within 12 months.

Morty was wonderful and encouraged me to live my life to the fullest, and I did. My life was filled with friends and all the activities one would expect in Manhattan. Mornings were busy with shopping sprees to Saks, Bloomies, or Manhattan boutiques, eyeing and often buying the latest fashion, even to the point where our apartment had to be renovated to add a wonderfully enormous walk-in closet. The hunt for trinkets included visits to Tiffany's and Cartier. Friends or I would reserve a table for lunch at Longchamps or The Plaza's Oak Room. Depending on the day of the week, afternoons were reserved for the hairdresser or a matinee. Evening schedules, too, were arranged well in advance and found Morty and me dining out, followed by concerts or the theatre. For years running I saw nearly every play on and off Broadway. Carnegie Hall and Lincoln Center were a source of constant delight.

I took up golf. In the spring and summer my schedule changed as I drove four times a week to the Saxon

Woods Golf Club in Scarsdale, to perfect my game. To make my one-hour journey pleasant and comfortable I was given a gift of a new convertible automobile. Socializing in the clubhouse or being chauffeured in a friend's limo followed hours on the course. On non-golfing days I took up another newfound hobby, ornithology. I enjoyed visiting a special section of Central Park on 77th Street. It was called The Rambles, a place where migratory birds would seek rest before continuing their flight.

Outwardly it seemed, at least to me, and probably to friends and family, my life was progressing normally. Life was like a grand waltz. But my inner life was not so joyful. I began to sense a semblance of unraveling, what I term a fraying of the spirit. I did not know why I felt this way, but I sensed somehow that it had to do with an imbalance between the fullness of my outward social life, and the lack of substance in my inner being. It felt like my spirit was being stretched to the breaking point. Neither Morty nor my mother were aware of it, nor, apparently, were my circle of friends, or they would have shown some concern. But I certainly sensed it. I became more and more distraught. In fact it progressed to the point where I was afraid to be alone.

It was a short time later that my mother and sister began to notice that things were not right, that I was becoming less and less rational in my behavior. I began to exclude friends and family from my daily routines. In fact they feared for me every time I was alone. Both mother and Adele tried to help me and made appointments with doctors recommended to them. They would accompany me, this to ensure that I would follow through with the appointments, but also to hear first hand the analysis and prescribed treatment.

Reading had always been an important part of my life. Now it became an escape - it became an excuse for not participating in family events or those scheduled by my friends. I remember reading the words of the sixteenth century essayist Michel Eyquem De Montaigne who wrote; "I know what I am fleeing from, but not what I am in search of." Although written almost 500 years ago, the words were ever present in my mind. I was a soul seeking to abandon my past, an effort begun when I was a child.

Selma remained with mother following my marriage to Morty. Without her daily presence I began to feel abandoned, and that led to my downward spiral, the cause for my breakdown. Morty was extremely kind, and a wonderfully, supportive husband. Yet my spirit was unsettled. I saw mother regularly, each week, but her lack of love for me was still always evident.

My condition worsened. Mother and Morty spoke to yet another New York neurologist about my condition. Pills of various sorts were prescribed; I took pills before breakfast and after breakfast. Other pills were taken midmorning, before lunch and after lunch. They were administered again in the afternoon and evening, and so it was for weeks on end.

During this period my mental health continued to deteriorate to the point where it became unsafe for me to be left alone; in fact a nurse was hired to ensure my personal safety. She was with me constantly. I was no longer free to even visit my favorite stores or restaurants without her shadow being constantly above or behind me. Social activities with friends that had been so much a part of my life became a thing of the past. I broke every friendship I had. All that was left for me in life were Morty, my mother, and my sister Adele. As necessary as those relationships were, I withdrew from them and crept deeper into my own cocoon.

It was only much later, long after my struggle with panic disorder that I understood how fragile I really was. I learned how my emotional abuse, some self-instilled, but mostly the result of my mother's painful rejection of me, had caused me to dismiss my own emotions. My heart ached but my consciousness did not understand why.

I became emotionally dysfunctional. I kept my pain hidden because I did not know how to express my anguish. My delusion of being in control had broken down and there were no resources left within me to move me toward normality. I was like a picture without a frame – without structure, without focus. Psychologically ill, I was completely frustrated by not understanding why I was so emotionally depressed when my life was so seemingly rich. I had a wonderful and devoted husband, a life full of socially rewarding and exciting activities, and a beautiful home near Riverside Drive. A neutral observer would have called my life fulfilled.

After a year of treatment it became obvious to Morty and mother that my diet of pills and weekly visits to doctors were not helping. The weekly sessions had not brought even a modicum of comfort. It was finally recommended that I be institutionalized at Blythewood.

The evening following the doctor's recommendation I packed my bags and Morty bundled me up for the 1 ½ hour drive to Greenwich, Ct. where Blythewood was located. It was a rainy, gloomy night, and darkness enveloped Greenwich as we pulled into the winding Blythewood driveway. We entered the pillared front entrance of the three stories Victorian manor house where I was ushered into the doctor's office. I sensed that the staff was very kind, even though they peppered me with questions. After the interview, I was escorted to my bedroom, said goodbyes to Morty and mother, then collapsed on my bed and began a crying bout that lasted weeks. It was a steady rivulet of tears…

It was during this period that I again opened my mind to the possibilities of God. I sought God's healing by giving up control of my feelings. I was unable to make sense of my emotions. It was one maudlin day followed by another. I knew that serenity would come only if I gave my will over to His control.

Joel S. Goldsmith taught:

> The secret of harmonious living is the development of spiritual consciousness. In that consciousness, fear and anxiety disappear, and life becomes meaningful with fulfillment as its keynote.

I had not yet read Goldsmith's works or taken to heart or assimilated his teaching that one must relinquish dependence on the external world of form, and place faith and confidence in something greater than ourselves, in the Infinite. I had not yet learned or comprehended that His grace was my sufficiency. I began to realize that I had to experience God within me, in my soul. I began to understand that as we seek peace within, we find harmony without. Goldsmith wrote, "We then have achieved the freedom of the Soul, the freedom of grace."

It was at Blythewood that I met a wonderful man, Dr. Percy R. Vessie.

On a pile of books near my bed at home is C.S. Lewis' *The Four Loves*. He writes about the most common and powerful human experience: need. He describes "need-based" love, and shares how that need is spiritual in nature because it draws us to God.

Dr. Vessie, my teacher and guide at Blythewood helped instill in me my seeking for "need-based" love. He was the instrument God used in helping me find Him. As my eyes swept the grounds of Blythewood from my bedroom window, I first saw him as he was walking along a path on the campus. My first impression was "this is a man unlike any I have seen before." It was almost as though he came from another planet; he was on a different plane from any person I had ever met. I felt a sense of him being illumined, from another dimension. I could not comprehend what he was. I had never met anyone like him.

## Chapter 3

### The Longing Heart

***"We may seek God by our intellect, but we only can find him with our heart." Cotvos***

Dr. Vessie was in charge of my case, and he found it most challenging because I was unable to communicate with him. In my condition I was unable to talk, and consequently, he was unable to conduct any semblance of psychoanalysis. I cried constantly in my discontent and I was extremely weak. Actually, I was terrified to live but also afraid to die. I was given a variety of vitamins to keep me physically well, but nothing could relieve my depression and I cried steadily for four months. My petulance became ever more apparent.

In an attempt to bring about a change in my condition and help me sleep, a series of drugs were added to my daily vitamin intake. I refused to talk with anyone or allow anyone to enter my room. The only thing I permitted the clinic to do was to deliver my food tray three times a day. So I lay there in my room for four long months watching the second hand on my clock slowly move the minutes to hours, watching daylight slowly transform into night. I was given a very strong drug, paraldehyde, to help me sleep. Dawn would herald another day in which the process would be repeated. I remember how the other patients complained about the drug's noxious odor and the smell that permeated the entire wing.

My initial months at Blythewood were frightening. The institution's staff, and even fellow patients were extremely intrusive. My impression was that staff and patients alike were spies. They reported every move I made and every move I didn't make to the chief doctors. Unknown to me, all of my activities were monitored and recorded through one-way glass. Even the letters I wrote to my husband and friends were opened and read prior to being mailed. Some were even returned to me and I was forbidden to mail them. In fact, a postcard I had written to my husband, pleading with him to come and take me away from that place, was handed back to me, and I was asked to explain how I could possibly criticize or fault Blythewood. Dr. Vessie's conclusive opinion was that I was totally dependent, emotionally, on Morty.

Dr. Vessie talked to me daily and asked how I was doing. I always replied the same way; "I'm terrified!" Identifying the source of that fear, however, was difficult and painful for me. It seemed as though the collective consciousness of the world -- the fear of the world -- had taken over my mind. I recall he said, "You must prepare for every eventuality of the mind."

Alone in my room I would hear an inner voice saying, "We have a big job here," or "This won't be simple, we have a lot to do." I also had visions of grapes and trucks, symbols of fruition and movement. Were these signs that God was moving in my unconscious...moving me toward a state of healing and fruition?

In an attempt to motivate me to communicate in some fashion, the staff had placed magazines, newspapers, and books in my room, but to no avail. Weeks and weeks went by until one day, my resistance waning, I picked up a notebook and wrote the words of the song, Tit-Willow, from Gilbert & Sullivan's, Mikado.

On a tree by a river a little tom-tit
Sang "Willow, tit-willow, tit-willow"
And I said to him, "Dicky-bird, why do you sit
Singing 'Willow, tit-willow, tit-willow'"
"Is it weakness of intellect, birdie?" I cried
"Or a rather tough worm in your little inside"
With a shake of his poor little head, he replied
"Oh, willow, tit-willow, tit-willow!"

He slapped at his chest, as he sat on that bough
Singing "Willow, tit-willow, tit-willow"
And a cold perspiration bespangled his brow
Oh, willow, tit-willow, tit-willow
He sobbed and he sighed, and a gurgle he gave
Then he plunged himself into the billowy wave
And an echo arose from the suicide's grave
"Oh, willow, tit-willow, tit-willow"

Now I feel just as sure as I'm sure that my name
Isn't Willow, tit-willow, tit-willow
That 'twas blighted affection that made him exclaim
"Oh, willow, tit-willow, tit-willow"
And if you remain callous and obdurate, I
Shall perish as he did, and you will know why
Though I probably shall not exclaim as I die
"Oh, willow, tit-willow, tit-willow"

This poor little bird needed love, but died without finding it. The words came to me from my subconscious and that's why I wrote them. So when Dr. Vessie came into my room he grabbed the writing pad because it was my first communication in all those many weeks. But the words meant nothing to him. To me, on the other hand, I was really sharing what my problem was. Dr. Vessie was wonderfully patient and understanding, although he did not comprehend what I was experiencing.

I saw in the song of suicide my own condition. However, unlike Tit Willow's song of despair, mine was to be a song of hope. Mine was to be a promise of peace and harmony to those who suffer with a "poor spirit". My spirit was rejuvenated. I was given a second chance when I placed my faith for living outside myself, in the loving grace of God. I placed it consciously in my soul where He resides.

Dr. Vessie was eager to solve my case but perplexed on how to treat me. He was in regular contact with my New York City doctor, writing him regularly, seeking his input to find a medical breakthrough. After weeks of probing and contemplating various forms of treatment, he decided to begin a 12-day treatment of daily insulin injections. Following the injections I was to remain in bed for 1 ½ hours. Then I was given a drink, which I believe was orange juice, to stave off insulin shock. Dr. Vessie also advised me, should anyone ask about this treatment, to be sure and explain to them "you never went into shock. I always took you 'out' before shock could occur."

After the injection I would perspire profusely for an hour and a half, then someone would come in and give me the drink. He told me the purpose of the series of injections was to change the pattern of my brain cells.

When the twelve-day insulin treatment was completed I suddenly heard a voice within me. The voice repeated the "Sermon on the Mount." I heard it over and over.

*Blessed are the poor in spirit, for theirs is the kingdom of heaven.*
*Blessed are those who mourn, for they will be comforted.*
*Blessed are the meek, for they will inherit the earth.*
*Blessed are those who hunger and thirst for righteousness, for they will be filled.*
*Blessed are the merciful, for they will be shown mercy.*
*Blessed are the pure in heart, for they will see God.*
*Blessed are the peacemakers, for they will be called sons of God.*
*Blessed are those who are persecuted because of righteousness, for theirs is the kingdom of heaven.*
*Blessed are you when people insult you, persecute you and falsely say all kinds of evil against you because of me.*
*Rejoice and be glad, because great is your reward in heaven...* Matthew 5: 3-12

No one had given me any forewarning that this phenomenon might occur. The words were repeated again and again... strangely, they brought an inner peace – calming – soothing my spirit. I felt the catharsis in my consciousness.

The words of Matthew's Fifth Chapter came to me four months after I was admitted to Blythewood. As I reflected on those words, unknown to me until I heard them being recited in my subconscious, it became clear that God was responding to my search for peace – He was responding to my soul, one very "poor in spirit."

Dr. Vessie asked me the following morning, on his next visit, the familiar question, "Well, kid, how are you doing?" I forced a wan smile and replied, "Either I'm a saint or I'm crazy!" I told him about the voice inside me that, following the two-week treatment, kept reciting the words of Jesus. He asked me, "Is the voice speaking *to you* or is it speaking *in you*?" "In me," I said, "but it's so fast! It takes my breath away!" He told me he'd slow it down for me, which he did. How he did it will always be a mystery to me.

Dr. Vessie visited me every morning. On one of these visits I wore my new dress, purchased from another resident at Blythewood. There was a knock on the door and Dr. Vessie entered. He smiled and asked, "And how are you today?" I later learned that he knew exactly how I was. He had learned clairvoyantly what had happened to me, and he had in fact dashed directly up from his cottage to confirm it. Of course I didn't know that at the time he already knew. I replied in a very dignified way, "I have a new technique now".

"And what might that be?" he asked. I told him animatedly that I had found a new place within myself where the fears and terrors couldn't get in. I recall seeing the sparkle of excitement in his eyes. He of course knew, whereas I did not, the meaning of what had happened to me. I had been opened to God's presence in me following the insulin injections. My resistance had waned and my defenses were crumbling.

Nearing the end of the four months I suddenly found a place within myself where the fear and the terror, which had been so prevalent in my consciousness, could not enter. It was a calm and quiet place protected from any intrusion. I could not believe that this had happened! When I was in that special place, fear or negative emotions could not trespass. It was quite possible to visit, to hide, and to live there. I didn't understand what the place was, but I now know that it was the Kingdom of God, that inner sanctum where He abides.

It was from that place that God shared, through Jesus' Sermon on the Mount, a foretaste of where the eternal Kingdom would be. It was in that place where the Voice had a home and from where it emanated to lift my spirit. I was very, very happy about God bringing me to it.

That very day a good friend of Dr. Vessie's, from Temple Rodeph Sholem, New York, came to visit him. They were together later that day as I happened to pass by and he grabbed hold of me and said to his friend, "I want you to meet this kid." He called all his patients kids. I was 25 years old at the time. He continued, "She has a very evolved nervous system. It's very highly developed." He proudly showed me off. And he told me later that the insulin treatment he had prescribed would only have had such positive results in someone with a highly developed nervous system, and that it was the insulin that allowed this special "place" to become unblocked. He said that in patients who were less evolved the results would not have been the same. That I had begun hearing voices long before was another sign that the treatment was working, that my "inner center" was open to my consciousness. I was a new person! I now had this "private sanctuary" within where I could always go to find solace.

When I returned to New York my friends and family would say to me, "You are different, there's something new and unique about you! You are like a new person. What happened to you up there?" Before my Blythewood treatment I had become steadily more socially dislocated.

"Nothing," I would reply. I really didn't know what to say, so that was my ready response.

Ever since that time, I have known where I could go to meet God and find solace, knowing God and I are One. I believe that God created my soul so that I would have a secret place where we could commune and be One. To experience God in this way became particularly meaningful. It was not just belief that moved me to God; it was the experience of God Himself within me. I am convinced beyond any doubt that my soul is filled with His Presence and that no power exists that could penetrate or in any way threaten my God experience. Spiritual healing was a necessary part of my healing process. I needed to have my soul revealed to me in order to begin to understand who I was. I needed to experience inner healing; a healing that can only come about through communion with the Eternal.

Joel Goldsmith said,

> "Man will find that even when all physical, mental, moral, or financial discords have been eliminated there will still be an inner unrest. Man will still not

> be at peace with himself… even were you healed of every physical or mental ill at this moment, even if your economic situation or personal relationships were entirely to your satisfaction, there would still be unrest within, and a discontent…"

Harmony in life is only found when one accepts God's gift of peace. Although not a Christian I was familiar with certain New Testament passages. One that spoke to my heart during my Blythewood stay was, "Come to me, all you who are weary and burdened, and I will give you rest… you will find rest for your souls…" (Matt. 11: 28-29. As I meditated on the words of Jesus I felt the realization of God's presence and power.

Joel wrote,

> "Spiritual healing is the touch of the Spirit of God in man's Soul; and when that touches him, it awakens him to a new dimension of life, a spiritual dimension: 'Where the Spirit of the Lord is, there is liberty' … because the Spirit of the Lord lifts the seeker into a new consciousness of life, the state of consciousness which the Master described as 'My kingdom' which is not of this world. When man attains that state of consciousness, he lives in a dimension of life other than the three-dimensional one, and he has experiences totally unknown on the human level of life."

I had not yet met Joel Goldsmith or his writings, but Dr. Vessie was leading me unknowingly, while I was his patient, toward God's teachings through Joel. I was finding God in my spiritual experience at Blythewood. It was hallowed ground.

# Chapter 4

## A Perspective from Above

**But those who hope in the LORD will renew their strength. They will soar on wings like eagles; they will run and not grow weary, they will walk and not be faint.**
Isaiah 40:31

Top on the "must see" list of many visitors to New York City is its world famous Central Park, one of the urban wonders of the world. In addition to hosting tourists from every corner of the world, it is a place of solace for thousands of New Yorkers. The park is a green oasis nestled amidst buildings stretching like giant fingers to the sky, and surrounded by bustling streets and sidewalks. It is so naturally a part of the Manhattan environment that many people do not realize it is entirely man-made.

The park caters to pleasure seekers of every age and taste. There are open-air concerts, strolling minstrels, kiosks offering up ice cream or roasted chestnuts. The baseball diamonds number more than I care to count. Paths for joggers, bicyclists, and now, even roller bladers circle and crisscross the park. For those simply wishing a stroll, meandering paths wind through the trees and across the meadows. The paths trail through glens and along the many ponds and the small lake. The lake wraps around an area called the Rambles where shade and peninsulas have been created to offer respite to strolling visitors and winged friends. The name's genesis sprang naturally from the chief activity of those visiting there, rambling.

The Rambles' open woodland thickets harbor more than 250 species of birds, many making their migratory flights in April and October on the Atlantic flyway. The Rambles has been rated one of the top 15 bird watching sites in the entire United States. Trees dating from the Ramble's planting now populate this woodland. One of the most famous – a tupelo –fells its leaves in autumn and they turn a brilliant ruby red. Winter brings a blanket of snow and frozen ponds, beckoning Manhattan high-rise sophisticates to search their closets for cross country skis and figure skates.

On my return to New York City from Blythewood, I understood that my soul needed further healing. I realized that I needed to break from the frenetic pace and life style I had led prior to my Blythewood stay. The Rambles, where I had first taken up my hobby, ornithology, seemed the perfect place to seek a fuller harmony with God and I went there regularly to be refreshed and find peace.

The Rambles was only a short distance from my home and I began to visit regularly. I would dash off directly after breakfast, grabbing my binoculars and a sandwich, to join with my group of friends, those I had enjoyed so much prior to Blythewood. I was so happy to see them again and I will never forget their kind welcome on my return.

Among the more common birds found at the Rambles were seagulls. This was not very strange at all since it was only a short flight for them to Central Park, whether coming from the East River or the Hudson River. They knew from earlier visits that the steady stream of visitors would bring scraps of food to answer their frenzied screeches.

Most of those in our "regular" bird watching group, those coming to observe and study the migratory flocks, paid little attention to the gulls' signals. We were focusing binoculars on the more colorful and exotic birds, flying in, then resting on the lake to regain strength before setting off again. One morning, however, there was one seagull that caught my attention.

As I watched the gull, I was fascinated by the odd way it was hopping and flapping its right wing. Was it trying to fly? Was it performing some silly pivotal courtship dance? The other seagulls seemed to ignore it. They simply took a step or two, and with a simple flap of their wings, off they went flying higher and higher. But this gull, no matter how hard it tried, was unable to lift itself from the ground.

There were perhaps 12 or 13 in our group of amateur ornithologists, and all were by now captivated by the bird's strange antics. We began speculating as to the gull's plight, "could it have a broken wing, are the feet damaged, has it been shot by a young boy's slingshot?"

Replacing his binoculars in its leather case, one of our members slowly approached the bird, searching his pockets as he drew near. I remember how the group's chatter lowered to a hush when he pulled out a knife.

The seagull made a frantic but futile attempt to fly away. My friend moved quickly and scooped up the bird, holding it securely under his left arm. For the next several minutes he flicked his little pocketknife into its feathers and around its feet. We thought that our friend was trying, as gently as possible, to put the bird out of its misery. But why was it taking so long?

Then the strangest thing happened. To the amazement of the entire group, our friend tossed the bird high into the air. At first the bird seemed as startled as we were, but then it began to flap its wings, and as the air caught underneath them it was able to fly off to join the rest of the flock.

Our friend approached us as he put away his little penknife and then opened his other hand for all to see, revealing a small bundle of translucent thread. We recognized it immediately as fishing line. The bird had become entangled in the fishing tackle used by one of the many children who came daily to fish at the lake. Our friend had come to its rescue and loosened its bonds saving it from a slow but certain death.

As I walked home some hours later, I reflected on the similarity in the plight of that little bird and my own condition some months earlier. I had also been ensnared and unable to free myself and had frantically sought release. But in so doing became more entangled, bound tightly by invisible, subconscious forces from which I could not free myself. Then God came to my rescue. He lifted me gently in His arms and there, ever so slowly, one strand at a time, He cut me free and said, "You're free to fly again."

God had not only set me free, He ignited my spirit. He had sprung up in the depth of my being with a yearning for me to know more about His love. I was not sure where to begin this search for a closer communion with God, but I believed it would likely be found and sustained in a spiritual fellowship. But I had very little experience with fellowships, churches, and temples. I had never really been a religious person. All I knew was that, like David, *"I love the Lord because He heard my voice and my supplications. He inclined His ear unto me, therefore I will call on Him as long as I live."*

My search for God had been answered. Now the search for a deeper love experience must begin.

As I pondered my next step I began to reflect on these two words, religious and spiritual. In my mind, my experience was more spiritual than religious, that is, God had blessed my searching with spiritual experiences. A religious experience in my mind translated as less personal, less searching, less invasive, less committed. My experience with God at every transcendental juncture in life had been very personal, in fact, mystical. God, sensing my sense of inadequacy to the stresses and strains of life had come to my rescue, and I had begun taking small but deliberate steps of faith.

I remember reading the words of an old saint who said, "Holiness can't be rushed." There is no sudden triumph to spiritual maturity. Spiritual growth is a work of the moment, one moment at a time. It was God and I working alone. None-the-less, I felt that further spiritual growth might come through collective worship.

I had found peace within and now I felt I had also to find a harmony without. I had always had that harmony with Morty. If ever there were soul mates, we were those souls. We were one. However, I sensed God leading me to a greater harmony in the world. I had cut myself off completely from many of my closest friends. I felt that I needed to find a spiritual plateau on the mountain of faith that I was climbing, a plateau on which I could rebuild my relationships, this time on a deeper spiritual plane.

Morty, my guide and life partner for nearly 67 wonderful years, became my helper in seeking answers to my need for a deeper spiritual understanding We began a weekly journey in search of a spiritual home, a home where my new found faith could grow and strengthen. Our Sunday journeys brought us to a series of churches in Manhattan and beyond. Our search continued for months, but I never sensed that I was being brought closer to God through the many visits. After all, if God was within me, was there really a need to search outside of myself? The author of Second Peter says as much by affirming God's promises to call us to God's "own glory and excellence to the extent that we become partakers of the divine nature." (2 Peter 1:3-4) St. Paul wrote in his letter to the Christians in Ephesus, " There is one God and Father of all mankind, who is Lord of all, works through all, and is all."

After almost a year of Sundays, Morty and I agreed that there were only two churches that we would consider for future visits. (Morty and I were Jewish, of course, but this had little bearing on our decision at the time.) Not far from our home, Riverside Church was one of our choices. The Rev. Dr. Harry Emerson Fosdick was the Pastor during our many visits, and he remained there through the Second World War, until 1946. He was a wonderfully gifted speaker and Morty and I learned a great deal from his teaching, particularly about the New Testament and Jesus Christ. It was there that my trust in Jesus became grounded. I recall singing a hymn there that remains a favorite even today, 60 years later. The author, Horatio Stafford was no stranger to pain and adversity. He lost most of his personal possessions in the Chicago fire of 1871.

Two years later he lost four daughters at sea, and a son just a few years after that heartbreak. Yet, he wrote in faith,

*When peace like a river attendeth my way.*
*When sorrows like sea billows roll.*
*Whatever my lot, thou hast taught me to know*
*It is well, it is well with my soul.*

*My sin –O, the bliss of this glorious thought-*
*My sin – not in part, but the whole,*
*Is nailed to the cross, and I bear it no more,*
*Praise the Lord, Praise the Lord, O my soul.*

*It is well with my soul*
*It is well, it is well with my soul.*

And so it was, it was well with my soul.

The second church we enjoyed attending regularly was The Marble Collegiate Church, also in Manhattan.

Again, we were greatly inspired by a great orator and preacher, the famous Dr. Norman Vincent Peale. His preaching, which regularly focused on the power of the individual and positive thinking, seemed to be God-inspired and often directed specifically to me. Strangely, I think, it was to a great degree Dr. Peale's preaching that prompted me to re-think whether God's plan for me included communal worship. I pondered following my very personal God experience, that perhaps worship in a community or fellowship was not necessary, it could even be a detriment to my spiritual growth. Every recollection of my spiritual history was a transcendental, personal and private encounter with the Infinite.

My unconscious continued to unfold, and my search turned to the Eastern religions. I concentrated all my energies on seeking the Truth. One day a friend, Ralph Houston gave me a little book that spoke directly to my soul, *The Masharshi's Gospel*, published in Madras, India, in 1939. Embodied in these pages were answers to everything I had been yearning to know. Because there was only one copy in print available to me at that time, I was impelled to copy the whole book down in longhand so I would never have to part with the words of this illumined Master. I cannot count how many times in my life I have re-read this little book.

Sometime later, another writing crossed my path that I knew at once was the next step for me. Written by an Indian sage, Sri Aurobindo, it was entitled *Integral Yoga*. I carried it with me for three years, reading and re-reading it until *Integral Yoga* became an integral part of my consciousness. When I felt that this had really happened – that it had taken root – I was ready for the next step, although I didn't know what form it would take.

Surprisingly, my search would turn to another direction.

As much as I enjoyed and believed in the teachings of Eastern mystics and sages, none of the Eastern religions gave me the answer for which I was seeking. It did not provide the steady and continual healing I so desperately sought.

In my search I visited a psychic in New York City who told me, "There is a man sending you love. He will be your spiritual teacher. You don't know him – but he will lead you on your journey for truth." I replied, "I don't want to be tied down to any spiritual teacher." She said, "He won't tie you down at all." I had no reason to believe, or not to believe, this woman. But the psychic's words would soon take on a new significance.

I was strolling Manhattan and decided to visit a favorite bookshop, The Gotham Book Mart, nestled between two high-rise office buildings at 41 West 47th Street. I felt I had absorbed all I could from the *Integral Yoga*. I was not looking for any particular author or book and simply browsed the shelves. At random, I picked up a book entitled *The Infinite Way*, by Joel Goldsmith. Perusing the pages, I knew that this was the spiritual teacher my psychic had told me about. The book opened itself to a page where there were quotations from every Indian master, every mystic that I had studied and had learned so much from. When I saw that Joel Goldsmith had been a Christian Science practitioner for 18 years and had studied all the same people that I had studied, I knew he was the one for me. I held the book up high and said, "This is it!" I couldn't wait to begin reading and studying the words – I knew they were written especially for me.

As soon as I arrived home I began reading, but realized immediately that the thoughts and insights were beyond my depth of understanding. I was still too intellectual and the book was written for someone who had the spiritual discernment to understand or apprehend the transcendental. I sensed that with time, the riches of Goldsmith's teachings and directions would become clear, therefore I carried the book with me, as I had done with Aurobindo's *Integral Yoga*, studying and meditating on his words at every opportunity. My faith was rewarded, but not through studying the book alone.

Joel Goldsmith lectured and conducted classes all over the world for years, and finally his classes were recorded. I sent for his cassette tapes, and for eight years I listened alone in my den to the tapes that arrived from Hawaii, where he lived. I listened to them over and over again until they became a part of my consciousness.

After eight years of listening, studying and meditating on his words I wrote Joel and asked if he would accept me as a private student. I was privileged to meet and learn at the feet of the author in both public and private visits, from California to Chicago to New York. Our meetings were remarkable in many ways, not least in my learning how similar our paths to God were. Joel served God years before he knew Him, as I had. Joel's search led to many sources seeking answers, and often believing he had found fulfillment, as did my search. However, it was not until after more than four decades of seeking that Joel experienced his "transition", in1946. And so it was for me. .

Joel Goldsmith once shared that I was one of his top students. His compliment referred both to my willingness to absorb the *Infinite Way* message, and also to the fact that I became a committed disciple. Joel wrote in his latter years, "You can never succeed because God is the only activity, but you can be the instrument for God's work. You can be the instrument for God's labor; you can be the instrument for God's love…."

**Never Apart**

**Take away the movie and what is left? The screen.**
**The screen –**
**And there - projected –**
**Is the moving picture scene (seen).**
**So, God,**
**Behind the drama**
**Of my human life since birth**
**Projects as me**
**To live as He**
**My life upon this Earth.**

Evelyn Brill Stark

Joel's message became my message, and I worked tirelessly for many years distributing his message via books and audio recordings throughout the world. I recorded an audiocassette wherein I shared my violin playing, my poetry and my writings.

My stepping-stones of learning had brought me to an awareness of my own spirituality and to Joel.

Joel Goldsmith wrote this in *The Master Speaks*, teaching me on searching for God:

> Begin with this simple practice; first, find out *what* God is; then, find *where* God is. When you find God to be the consciousness of your own being, when you find that God is your very consciousness, your very awareness; you will have found all the forms as which God appears. You will then find God unfolding Itself - Consciousness unfolding Itself, revealing Itself - as your daily experience.
>
> Never forget this: that which appears as our daily finite experience, is our sense of limitation, appearing as a lack of education, or lack of opportunity, or lack of a satisfactory environment. All of that is appearing as our limited daily experience. When, however, we begin to realize this great truth of being, that we are not limited to the finite sense of consciousness, that we are not limited to our personal sense of existence; but rather that God, the infinite consciousness of our being is the source and form of our life; then, watch the miracles that begin to occur in our experience.

I included in my search audiotapes of Joel Goldsmith. He warned the new believer to be aware of what might happen. It was tape #86, recorded in 1954:

> For a number of reasons, the new Christian fails to maintain the enthusiasm that once led to obedience. Perhaps it was a lack of supporting structure around

> the new convert or too much of an opposing influence from friends, relatives or co-workers that caused the reversal on their initial decision to become a Christian. For whatever reason, the new Christian now becomes passive, that is to say, they are no longer active nor do they attend worship, pray, or perhaps keep their covenant with God concerning the items they once repented of. This is a dangerous situation.

My visits to Dr. Vessie continued many years following my healing at Blythewood. He often reminded me of the words God had imprinted on my subconscious at Blythewood, "Blessed are the poor in spirit." That had been my condition, the one from which God lifted me. It was a personal spiritual craving, one with but one answer, an answer I found within me. I learned that for me to grow spiritually I needed to search privately, within, not collectively in community. Both Dr. Vessie and Joel Goldsmith taught me this.

Thomas Merton has always been a favorite mystic teacher and I learned much from him about the contemplative life:

> Why do we think of the gift of contemplation, infused contemplation, mystical prayer, as something essentially strange and esoteric reserved for a small class of almost unnatural beings and prohibited to everyone else? It is perhaps because we have forgotten that contemplation is the work of the Holy Spirit acting on our souls through His gifts of Wisdom and Understanding with special intensity to increase and perfect our love for Him. These gifts are part of the normal equipment of Christian sanctity… it is also true

> that God often measures His gifts by our desire to receive them, and by our cooperation with His grace…
>
> God, then, has created us to share in His own life. He has given Himself to us as the very source of our being. Not only that, but He has chosen to dwell in this very being of ourselves and to give us a share in His own knowing and loving of all creation and all beings." Merton says, "There are thousands of Christians walking about the face of the earth bearing in their bodies the infinite God of whom they know practically nothing ... God does not manifest Himself to these souls because they do not seek Him with any real desire. ... But desire is the most important thing in the contemplative life."

My experience mirrored Merton's words. I do not believe everyone has a craving for "the search" in themselves, at least not to the point where it motivates them to seek God. They may have it in a dormant stage, but they are living a life that prevents it from coming to the surface. They are living their own way according to the way they were born and into what family, the way they were taught in school, and the culture that surrounds them. They live an existence that prevents God from revealing Himself and His plan for them because there is no room for Him to come through. They never have the interruption in life that I experienced. It is when reliance on external sources of authority or influence are abandoned. It is when the will gives over to an internal contemplative search for the leading of the Divine that God will reveal Himself.

Many people end up very unhappy, and very empty, and they don't know why. They do not realize that the only thing that will bring them true joy and fulfillment is the discovery of their own true identity, the self-completeness of it, the harmony of it, the beauty of it, the independence of it, the freedom of it, not needing anyone to make them happy. They confuse conscious, fleeting external happiness with internal, eternal joy.

They do not know that there is within each person a place of utter belonging to God the very essence of us which makes life worth living. The center of our being will never rest until it is consumed and filled by God. St. Augustine's words say it adequately; "The heart is restless until it finds its rest in God." Unfortunately, a great many people are out of tune with God's plan of harmony for the soul, they simply cannot hear. Others yet, hearing God's love song, tune out because they are not developed enough emotionally to realize that the only thing that will satisfy them is God's love.

My visits to the Rambles provided me ample time for meditation and reflection. My faith grew as I thought back to the years when He provided immediate and convincing answers to my private prayers, and also through the ongoing healing experience. I sensed more strongly each day that He was bringing me "home."

The flocks that gather at the Rambles in Central Park included more than 200 species of birds and I was fascinated by every one of them. There was so much to learn. It was shared with me that several species migrate from Canada flying as far as South America. When the weather begins to warm in the North they begin their long return flight to Canada, a distance of several thousand miles. This in itself I found extraordinary. More so, in my mind, was what I learned about their Canadian destination. The birds return to their place of birth, to the very nest in which they were hatched. How extraordinary that in their little minds God had instilled such homing senses. To think that God had programmed their sense of home so intuitively that they could wing more than a thousand miles to an area as vast as North America, to a land mass as large as Canada, to a specific dense forest, a particular tree, and finally, the very branch where 6 months earlier the bird took flight. God guides it back to its place of birth, its home.

I often reflected on that phenomenon during my visits to the park. To think that God had created within those tiny birds a sense of knowing of just where they were weaned, the place where they first flapped their tiny, growing wings. It was the place where the mother had pushed its young out of the nest for that first fledgling, frightful flight.

The Bible tells us that not a sparrow falls without God's knowledge. It also reminds us that we, His children, are more precious than any of His creation. Should it be so strange then that he guided me back to Him? It was God that brought me home again. It was God who brought me to myself. It was God who set me free to fly. Once free He guided my flight home until I found my rest in Him, within me.

**Illumination**

**Awakening**
**Suspended in Love**
**Brushed by Angel wings**
**Nestled in Contentment**
**Free!**

Evelyn Brill Stark

## Chapter 5

### Thou Art

**The Friend I could count on right from the start**
**You have won all the love and the trust in my heart.**
**You're the Friend Who is waiting whenever I call**
**And You break through the blocks of my subconscious wall**
**To lift and to heal all my heartaches and pain**
**With the Truth that restores me to Wholeness again.**
**Attuned to Your Love in surrender and prayer**
**My heart is at peace and I rest in Your care.**

Evelyn Brill Stark

Reflecting on my spiritual path, the stepping-stones that brought me to Grace are many. The uninitiated or non-illumined would call the path folly, and stepping-stones of faith absurd. However, in my reality they were both lifesaving and continue to be life giving. Grace is available to all but understood by few. Grace is constantly in the presence of everyone, however, my experience tells me that most people are not aware of it. They have not been told about it and consequently do not know where to take the first step. Some do not even know it exists.

Being unaware of Grace, or refusing to acknowledge its existence, does not exclude the truth of its presence. I could as easily suggest that the wind does not exist because I cannot feel its effect blowing through my hair on a calm summer eve. It would also be absurd to say that it does not exist because I do not give any thought to it. . I know from the summer holidays spent in Maine that although not a blade of grass bent to the wind, I had simply to turn toward the sea and observe the spread wings of the gulls as they floated effortlessly higher and higher, lifted by an unseen ocean breeze.

Grace is God's love for all his children no matter who they are, where they are, or what they do. Grace operates for everyone. However, the lesson of grace is a difficult one to learn. If you know it is there you can actually submit to it. It is always acting but many are not getting the benefit of grace because many are still trying to run their own life. It is basically a way of surrendering one's life to God and to let His grace guide one's life, but to get to that point takes a long time. How many people actually test it? They hear that it exists and then laugh at it, or they continue living their life without giving any thought to Grace or the obligation that follows.

Being on the path means being a beholder of Grace, its wonder and power. The beholder will follow the leading of God's Grace, go where it leads, do what it says. That is what being on the Path means. The path will differ for each follower but Grace will lead all.

My steps on the path were at first cautious, tentative. Somehow I sensed that God was releasing grace as though in fragments. I could not fully comprehend His plan, but I learned in time that Grace is a wellspring that bestows insight, power, and direction in degrees. God does not disburse His power in degrees, but we receive it in degrees. At just the right moment of need God places a stepping-stone on the path of the seeker to guide the pilgrim further upward.

A person of great humility, whose works became a series of stepping-stones, was Joel Goldsmith. It was through my persistent 8-year-long meditation of Joel Goldsmith's *The Infinite Way*, paired with other inspirational reading, that the wondrous life-giving love of God, His Grace, was revealed fully as a practical way of life.

In Joel Goldsmith's, *The Art of Meditation*, Part 1, he writes:

> Most men and women are convinced that there is a divine Power of some sort operating in human affairs; but they are not sure what it is, nor do they know how to bring this divine Presence and Power into their daily experience. There was a time when many of these people were content to believe in a God dwelling in a remote heaven, a God whom they would not meet until after death. In this practical age, very few are satisfied with that limited concept of God.
>
> The world is full of discord. The question is asked again and again: Why, if there is a God, does this God permit sin, disease, war, famine, and disaster? How can all these evils be, if God is good, if God is life, if God is love? How can there be that kind of a God *and* the horrors of human experience? People throughout all time have attempted to solve this riddle, but there is no solution; there is no answer except that the world has not known God. We can never for a moment believe that if people in this world had a realization of God, they would have discord and disharmony, too. Discord and disharmony come into our life because of

our ignorance of God. As we acquaint now ourselves with Him, we find the secret of harmonious existence.

People throughout all time have sought freedom, peace, and plenty; but their search has been primarily through the feverish activity of the human mind. Pleasure and satisfaction have been artificially created, and because of their artificiality, they are neither permanent nor real. Living out from the level of the mind, there must be a continuous round of new pleasures, new faces, and new scenes. There is rarely a truly joyous moment, nor are there periods of rest and relaxation.

Freedom, peace, and plenty are not dependent upon circumstances or conditions. Men have been free in chains; they have been free under slavery and oppression; they have found peace in the midst of war; they have survived floods and famine; they have prospered in periods of depression and panic.

Reading Joel's work I was reminded of a story written by a friend, a story of living under oppression, sometimes of our own doing. Being a writer and a poet, I am often moved by stories and analogies of others, a favorite source being the New Testament. It is replete with analogies and antidotes, many told by Jesus. In fact, more than one third of the stories told by Jesus were parables. My friend's modern day parable placed yet another stepping-stone in front of me:

The woman trudged through the narrow muddy track that would lead her to the village market vegetable stalls, still more than a mile distant. She was bent low under the weight of the large sack carried on her back. The steady rains made the weekly trek more difficult than usual. Adding to the discomfort of the journey was the traffic of trotting horses and passing ox carts, their drivers whipping their beasts to maintain their gait. All were racing to ensure the best market stall location in which to sell their goods. The spinning cartwheels splattered mud in all directions, much of it landing squarely on the head and hunched shoulders of the figure seeking to side step the countless puddles.

An approaching horse cart slowed as it neared the woman. The horses were reined in as the horseman leaned across the buckboard seat. He tipped his rain soaked woolen cap to the familiar figure that trekked weekly to the village market. "Why don't you join me in the wagon?" he offered.

It took every ounce of strength for the old woman to lift her bundle onto the cart. She accepted the helping hand of the driver as she seated herself. Once onboard she bent to lift her heavy burden and placed it back over her shoulder. She was grateful that her journey had been made easier, particularly as she observed the many others who made the weary journey by foot. Her heart went out to one woman in particular making her way on the side of the roadway. She, too, was carrying a heavy sack, but had in tow two rain sodden youngsters picking their way along the muddy track. For a brief moment she saw another's plight as worse than her own. Then she shifted her heavy burden to the other shoulder.

My experience, even subsequent to becoming one with the Infinite, was very similar to that of the woman in the cart. Maybe that is your experience, too. Shakespeare's words from Julius Caesar are often the woes of the new believer, "*The evil that men do lives after them.*" We are unable to let go of our burdens, the sins of our past. We have carried them within for so long and so far that we do not realize how psychologically and even physically debilitating our past can be. Remembrance of one's past sins can drain every ounce of strength at exactly the time when resources are most needed. We seek to step forward but progress is halted due the burdens weighing us down.

We need to remind ourselves of the words of the Psalmist,

> "As far as the east is from the west, so far has He removed our transgressions from us."

God's offer of salvation through His Son includes the assurance that the burdens of our past are lifted and thrown aside in the twinkling of an eye. In the same instance as salvation is offered, God's grace, His strength through His Holy Spirit, helps us to forgive ourselves. There is not a problem of the human soul that The Infinite can't meet and overcome. Every personality and circumstance was anticipated when God planned our redemption.

**Breakthrough**

**For me the play is over**
**For me the scenes are dead**
**I leave the past behind**
**And set my goals ahead.**
**My earthly tragic comedy**
**Fulfilled its destined span**
**According to its purpose**
**According to its plan.**
**And all my cast of characters**
**Have played their fated part**
**The ones that brought me happiness**
**The ones that broke my heart.**
**I paid the price of sacrifice**
**Transcended point of view**
**The Truth dispelled illusion**
**And now my world is new.**

Evelyn Brill Stark

Like St. Paul on the Damascus Road, I opened my heart and He spoke to me. Like St. Paul, I closed my eyes to the past so that my heart could see His reality, and I found and accepted my Messiah. He taught grace instead of law. That spoke to me of peace of heart and mind.

I have an absolute commitment to God and His teachings through Jesus. I live Jesus' teaching, His teaching of grace. The power to live in Christ is inspired by the Holy Spirit, in whom I abide. It is in the strength of the Holy Spirit that I live and serve. St. Paul said it this way, " It's not I that liveth but Christ that liveth in me" You have to come to God saying, "I don't have the answer- I give myself over to you." Peace, power, and purity are all found in Christ and we are in Him. Our only need therefore is to maintain communion with Him. St. Paul's words to the Athenian philosophers are recorded in the Acts of the Apostles, "For in him we live and move and have our being. As some of your own poets have said, We are his offspring."

In redemption terms God is the Father of those who are in Christ. This means we are His children by Grace. In resurrection terms, it is God the Holy Spirit that empowers us to live a new life. Both redemption and resurrection come to us by means of Grace.

A dear friend who I met in recent years shared his grandfather, Herbert Booth's words with me. In the chorus of one of his many songs are these words to remind us of this truth,

*Grace there is my every debt to pay,*
*Blood to wash my every sin away.*
*Power to keep me spotless day by day.*
*For me, for me!*

In the same instance that the past was removed Grace remained within me to give me power for living. He who dwells on high and set the stars in their courses came down to lift the burdens from my heart. Grace then cast those sins into fathomless space and my burden was forever lifted.

I learned and accepted that God's promised grace is my sufficiency. It was through my commitment to regular study and meditation that God revealed His twofold purpose in disbursing Grace. We need to remember that He never withholds from us what we need in every situation. In fact we are told to seek His direction in boldness, certain of His showering on us grace for every need and circumstance.

He giveth more grace
as our burdens grow greater,
He sendeth more strength
as our labors increase,
To added afflictions
he addeth his mercy,
To multiplied trials
he multiplies peace.

Annie Johnson Flint

Joel Goldsmith's words in *Practicing the Presence* tell us about Grace and its sufficiency. (Part 1):

> The secret of harmonious living is the development of spiritual consciousness. In that consciousness, fear and anxiety disappear, and life becomes meaningful with fulfillment as its keynote.
>
> The degree of spiritual consciousness which we attain can be measured by the extent to which we relinquish our dependence on the external world of form and place our faith and confidence in something greater than ourselves, in the Infinite which can surmount any and every obstacle. It is an awareness of the grace of God.
>
> There is a specific practice which will aid in the attainment of this spiritual consciousness. It is a practice which can be carried on throughout the day as

> the world crowds in upon us, reminding us that we need this or desire that. To every such insistent demand, let our answer be: "No, no. This is not what I need or want. *Thy* grace is my sufficiency, nothing else – not money, not marbles, only *Thy* grace." Let us learn to hold to that resolutely. If the need seems to be railway fare, rent, clothing, housing, or health, let us steadfastly acknowledge that our only need is His grace.
>
> Our work may require greater strength, greater knowledge, or greater ability than we seem to possess, or there may be greater demands made upon our purse than we can meet. Instead of accepting this apparent lack, let us remember, "He performeth the thing that is appointed for me...The Lord will perfect that which concerneth me," or some other scriptural passage. The human belief may be that there is a physical, mental, moral, or financial demand made upon us greater than our ability to fulfill; but the very moment we turn to that He that is within us, recognizing that He performeth that which is given us to do, He perfecteth that which concerneth us, a weight drops off our shoulders, and the sense of personal responsibility lifts.

It is said that we will have two great surprises when we reach heaven. The first is, "I made it!" The second is the many countless who approach and say, "Thank you. It's because of your not accepting cheap grace that I am here. You accepted the calling to discipleship. You were His disciple in my life"

In 1962, the time had come when I felt that I understood Joel Goldsmith's message so completely, as it had been revealed so far, that I ought to seek a private meeting with him. Further growth, in my mind, would only come about by studying with the master himself. Perhaps he would accept me as a private student? My spirit was fully restored and I was one with the Infinite but yet I realized I to attain to the next level required direct contact with Joel. Yes, this must be the next step!

I really ought to write to him, I thought. I rushed to find a taxi and traveled to 42nd Street and Fifth Avenue, the New York Public Library, to seek out his address. I was certain they would have a Hawaii telephone directory.

## Chapter 6

### I Jumped Across a Rainbow

**I jumped across a rainbow**
**And left my ego here**
**Exposed to its reality**
**As nothingness and fear.**

**I needed all my courage**
**To take that giant leap**
**For hypnotized in human dreams**
**My mind was fast asleep.**

**But when that rainbow beckoned**
**I walked right through the night**
**I jumped across the rainbow**
**And fell into the Light!**

Evelyn Brill Stark

The New York Public Library is a massive place -- the largest library in the world. The guard at the front door directed me to the reference room where telephone books from every state in the country were stored. Hawaii had become the $50^{th}$ US State just ten years earlier.

**New York Public Library**

I brought the Hawaii telephone white pages to the library's reference table. I was dressed in my fur coat and laid my gloves on the table beside me. . It took me only a few seconds to find Joel Goldsmith's address: Pawaa Station, Kaimuki Town, and Honolulu. The Kaimuki part of the address had an aura about it – I pictured this ancient Hawaiian village set high on a hill with palm trees and waves breaking on the distant shore.

I pondered if I should write while still in the library.

I found a seat at a table surrounded with people thumbing through reference books, feverishly jotting notes on yellow pads or whatever scraps of paper they found close at hand.

I had not given thought to when or from where I would write, but this seemed just as good a time and place as any. If I did not take the time now to write, I was afraid I might be forced to delay it for several days due to my very busy schedule. I had read Joel's works many times over and I had spent countless hours listening to his audiotapes in my study for more than 6 years. The tapes were being sent to me regularly, but I was very busy in my own way, committed to share with others the joy I had found within me, through music. Added to an already hectic round of events I was regularly attending classes conducted by other Goldsmith devotees.

I was sharing my love, God's love in fact, through music with patients in many New York hospitals. I played the violin, and my friend Bessie Smith accompanied me at the piano. I considered my playing an art, a sacred trust put upon me by God. I will never forget the music that we performed at the Manhattan State Hospital. When we arrived at the hospital we were escorted to the first of many wards in which we would perform.

Since no repertoire had been suggested to us, Bessie and I had decided that we would begin our recital by playing Fritz Kreisler's *Liebesfreud* (Love's Joy). I looked out over my music stand at the patients to discern their reaction, and was aghast to see that many of the patients had begun to cry. As our song of Joy unfolded, more and more patients joined the others in tears. It was clear our music had touched their souls.

Following our concert I felt compelled to share a portion of my own spiritual journey with Bessie. I told her about Joel Goldsmith and how I had found the source of my soul's release, but more than that, my eternal source of unspeakable joy. They were also found in Kreisler's Liebesfreud, God's love. I told of how when I lifted the violin to play in the hospital I prayed in silence, "I offer this gift of music through You, God. Is it any wonder then that God touched the souls of our listeners, His children?"

It was a surprise to me when a few days later, Bessie came to me and showed me a clipping from the New York Times in which there was an announcement about a Goldsmith public lecture and class being scheduled in New York City.

I read the small advertisement with excitement and immediately checked the date in my pocket diary to see if there were any conflicting engagements. I noted in my little book that Morty and I were already committed to a social event the same evening as Joel's lecture. This would be my first opportunity to see and hear Joel Goldsmith in person. I wondered if Morty would understand if I decided to attend the Goldsmith lecture instead of joining him.

When I got home I spoke immediately to Morty. I had no way to forecast his reaction. Our social commitment had been made weeks in advance. However, he knew how engrossed and captivated I was by the *Infinite Way* message, and having witnessed its healing powers in my life he reacted quickly, saying that he would go alone and in so doing make an appearance and represent us both.

I was determined to arrive at the lecture early enough to secure a seat with a good view of the podium without being too conspicuous. I found an aisle seat about half way down on the right hand side of the auditorium. My early arrival helped secure a good seat in what would soon be a standing-room-only crowd.

I remember to this day how very impressed I was by Joel's presence and message. I was amazed at his clarity and ability to impart instruction and guidance on such a deep and eternal subject. I really was not surprised though. After all, he was chosen by God to be His messenger. I heard comments from those seated near me,

"It's incomprehensible how he is able to share the Pathway so clearly." and, "His wisdom and ability to share is extraordinary." His voice was deep and soothing. His phrasing was like music, interspersed with just the right amount of humor.

Joel spoke for more than an hour and then decided to call a brief intermission. Clearly, it was Joel who needed a break – the audience was still seated as though spellbound by his message. He suggested that those who wanted to become more familiar with his teaching might want to purchase his books, or sign up for the classes to be conducted during the next five days. Those interested were invited to visit the bookstall in the hotel's foyer.

I remained seated while many in the audience moved from their seats, some to visit with friends, others to examine the books being offered for sale. The crowds moving up and down the aisle blocked my view of the auditorium's stage area. No doubt many were making their way to the front to see, and with luck, even meet Joel Goldsmith. When the crowd in the aisle in which I was seated began to clear I sensed someone standing near me. I looked up and there was Joel Goldsmith looking down at me.

"Good evening," he said, "and how are you tonight?"

I sat fixed to my chair, nonplussed. He turned before I could compose myself and reply to his simple and gracious greeting. Why, with so many hundreds assembled, would he choose to come just to me? I was confused and felt that in that I had not responded adequately. I needed to remedy my awkwardness in some way.

Joel had concluded the first part of his lecture with an invitation to those in the audience to attend the evening lectures scheduled for the coming week. But he made it clear who would actually be invited. . He said, "Most of you come to this message for healing in some form… Very few are here who want to go the whole way." Joel's long affiliation with Christian Science was well known, as was God's gift of healing through him.

People were still milling about the auditorium so I moved from my chair and went to the front to seek out Joel. I found him surrounded by a large circle of followers. I made my way through the crowd and stood in front of Joel. He turned to face me directly. I looked into his eyes, and said, **"I AM GOING THE WHOLE WAY,"** loud enough for all in the circle to hear. Then I turned abruptly and returned to my seat. I felt Joel's eyes following me.

When the lecture concluded, I joined a large crowd at the bookstall in the foyer. Joel approached the table and I had another opportunity to speak with him. Because his lecture had included many references to healing and Christian Science, I felt I needed to clarify my background prior to registering for his class. I said to him, "I don't know anything about Christian Science. Is that a hindrance?" Joel replied, "It's probably better that way…read my writings."

I purchased a copy of each book displayed on the table, and even those still in manuscript form. Enrolling, I paid $50 for the next 6 nights of lectures.

Each night as I departed the auditorium after attending Joel's class, my spirit danced in harmony with the Infinite. There was so much to absorb that I scarce could take it all in. As the week drew to a close I became more and more anxious about what was to be my next step.

I continued reading his works, listening to his recordings. I subscribed to and read his monthly newsletter, but my spirit had not fully understood what Joel was sharing. I yearned to understand more deeply what the Spirit was communicating.

My mind went back to the many lectures, and all the reading of the last 2 years as I pondered what to write… I put my pen to paper and wrote…

*February 9, 1961*

*Dear Joel,*

*I don't know if you remember me, but I met you in New York, when you conducted your classes here. I'm the person who came to you during the first lecture intermission and said, "I am going to go the whole way!"*

*I have attended every lecture you have conducted in New York, and devoted many hours each day to studying and meditating on The Infinite Way message. I have moved from stage to stage but now find myself in need of a personal and private teacher.*

*Will you be my teacher?*

*Sincerely,*

*Evelyn Stark*

I returned home from the library and fetched an envelope and a 7-cent stamp and airmailed the letter from a mailbox on Riverside Drive. I had to brush snow from the mailbox lid to open it. I remember thinking that I mustn't let any snow get on the envelope for fear that the address become smudged and the letter relegated to the "addressee unknown" bin. In a few days the letter would be in Hawaii, where palms and the Pacific Ocean meet. A far cry from wintry Manhattan…

Was my decision to seek a direct link with Joel Goldsmith the correct next step? I had made the mistake of tying myself too closely with spiritual teachers in the past. Was I doing it again?

I knew that it would take some days for my letter to reach the island state of Hawaii. With Joel's very busy schedule traveling to all corners of the globe, would he be in Hawaii to receive my letter? Even if he were, would he have time to respond to my plea for spiritual direction? I waited earnestly each day for the mailman's visit to our building, and asked our doorman to call me immediately on delivery of the day's mail.

The doorman buzzed our apartment on February 21, 1961 and said, "Your Hawaii letter is here!" I immediately took the elevator downstairs and there it was, a letter postmarked, Kailua, February 18, 1961. I tore open the envelope as I reentered the elevator and noted that Joel's letterhead included Aloha in the upper left hand corner. Joel Goldsmith's reply was finally in my hands.

*February 17, 1961*

*Dear Friend:*

*I am sure you know that it would be entirely out of place for me to give you advice on something as important as your spiritual welfare*

*For each of us who are serious seekers of spiritual life and law, there is a teaching and a teacher. But each one of us has within ourselves a divine instinct that tells us when we have found our teacher, or our teaching, and it is a very unwise thing to seek human advice on such a subject. No one but you can know when you have found that which is to bring your spiritual release. No one but you can know when you have found that which would make you able to fulfill the Master's words, "Leave all and follow me. Leave mother, brother, sister, father for My sake." Who could ever give you advice, or tell you when you have found that for which you would sacrifice the rest of the world?*

*I am very clear in my lectures and in my Classworks when I say to my students, or to those who come to hear, that it is unwise to come to this Message on someone else's advice, or because someone else had a healing. A Spiritual Path in life is not only an individual one, but it is a sacred one, and each person must find the one that is for them.*

*This is a matter for you to take into the innermost heart of hearts, the inner sanctuary of your own being, and commune with God until you receive an answer.*

*Aloha greetings,*

*Joel*

Joel's reply seemed to me somewhat of a rebuke. I had earnestly sought God's leading these many years. Years of searching had led me to God in my innermost heart, and Joel writes to tell me to go back there? Should I write Joel and explain further about where my spiritual Path had led me?

It was clear that Joel's letter meant to convey that I needed to search deeper within until God leads me to my next step.

In my reading during that period I decided to include stories from the Pacific islands. I suppose I was seeking to know why Joel, a New Yorker by birth, had chosen to settle in a place and culture so different from our own. Was he sent there?

I was drawn to stories from Hawaii, and came across one from folk history that suggests that a child comes into this world as a bowl of bright shining light. However, as the child begins to grow and develop, rocks are placed into the bowl. Before long as more and more rocks are added the rocks begin to block out the bright shining light emanating from the bowl's center.

Rocks added to the bowl are developed through anxiety; through fear; through bitterness; through jealousy; through human strife; through thoughts of inadequacy; of unworthiness. As the human traits are added the bowl becomes heavier and heavier, too heavy for the traveler to continue the journey. The many stones now weighing down the bowl smother the light. For the child to be nurtured and whole again, the rocks need to be removed until the center shines brilliant once again.

I wondered if I should write Joel again, perhaps sharing the story as a kind of opener – sharing with him that many rocks had been removed and that the Light within me had again begun to shine bright these last several years. I could tell him that I was ready for the next stage, knowing now that he was the only teacher that I wanted.

The Light has always existed in our center, our soul. Thomas Merton wrote, "Contemplation is a mystery in which God reveals Himself as the very center of our own inmost self." It is there where the Light of God will be found and known. It is in turning to the inward Light that one realizes that the Light will dissipate stones into dust that then is tossed to the winds. The Light breaks through and we become fulfilled and transformed. The Light becomes our present and our Presence.

I had found the Presence, the Light, within me. I had come from deep valleys of despair to an inner knowledge of the Eternal. Light had been revealed to me and I was at one with the Infinite.

One of the world's greatest and most beloved hymn writers, Fanny Crosby, penned these words as though for me…

*Do you ask what I found in this Valley?*
*'Tis my trysting place with the Divine,*
*For I fell at the feet of the Holy,*
*And above me a voice said, "Be Mine."*
*And there rose from the depth of my spirit,*
*The echo, "My heart shall be Thine."*

I continued meditating on Joel's works almost a full year before deciding to write to him again.

*New Year's Day, 1962*

*Dear Joel,*

*The feelings that prompt me to write this letter are of such purity, strength and urgency that they must come from God.*

*I have been with you for over 6 years now, studying the books, attending the classes – listening to the tapes, and it has been the blessing of my life. But now I feel a desire to be more closely identified with you – a closer relationship between us. I want you for my teacher in a more personal sense than you already are.*

*You said in one of your letters that you would do anything to help a student who cares deeply about getting on in this work. Believe me, I couldn't care more deeply.*

*My feeling for you Joel is of such a nature that you are the only person on earth to whom I could commit myself spiritually – with complete trust – and love. I have felt the need to go my way alone- an intense need for freedom and privacy.*

*The realization and experience of God came to me many years ago. Since then I have been trying to nurture it and absorb the metaphysical side of it into my consciousness. I study and practice, and very gradually it seems to me I am succeeding. But there is still a long way to go. And I mean to go the whole way.*

*Will you help me – as my teacher?*

*Deepest alohas,*

*Evelyn Stark*

I wondered if Joel would recognize that this was my New Year's resolution and prayer. His reply was long in coming. No doubt he was meditating on whether to accept me as a student. Then it came, Joel's reply…

*January 22, 1962*

*Dear Friend:*

*And now we embark on a great mission. When I undertake to lead a student to the realization of the kingdom of God, the student has every right to expect that I will give of myself to the fullest, and that I will not withhold time, effort, energy, or anything else that might be helpful to the student in arriving at their destiny.*

*Those who come to Infinite Way lectures or Classes I ask nothing of beyond their attention. I recognize that they are seekers, and that it is my function to present that which God has given to me to them, and that they have the right to accept as much or as little as their own capacity determines. However, once a student has recognized the teacher, and has set the foot on the spiritual Journey, then I ask as much of the student as the student has a right to expect of me.*

*Scripture calls this giving the first fruits to God. In practical experience it really means the utmost of our time, our attention, our devotion, our dedication, our consecration. It means always putting first things first, and yet never neglecting the honorable duties and obligations which are ours on the human plane.*

*As you undoubtedly know from the Monthly Letter, the first half of this year will be spent in two months of work in California, and about two weeks in Chicago, and then back here for Classwork in July. The balance of the year will be in Europe, middle and South Africa.*

*This means that if you can possibly be in any of our work in California, Chicago or Hawaii, that you will have the benefit of all the work that I do with our students, not only in the regular lecture and Classwork, but also in the work which is not scheduled in the Letters at all, and which is never mentioned.*

*And if it is not possible for you to attend any of that work, then our work will have to be conducted by mail.*

*My first suggestion is that you take the introduction to "Practicing the Presence" and spend several days just with that introduction, and then take the rest of the book slowly. At some other part of the day you can take the book "Living The Infinite Way" and take it slowly. This is merely in the nature of review, so that whatever is necessary to come to your conscious attention will be brought to light while you are working on these two books. Then, any questions that arise in your thoughts should be written to me.*

*Meanwhile, I conduct my work on the inner realm for you and with me.*

*Greetings of peace! Joel*

In opening Joel's letter I noticed that there was another page in the envelope. I unfolded it and noted that the page was filled with handwritten notes… it was a list of Joel's upcoming lectures. Five were scheduled for the spring of 1962 in California, one in Chicago, and one in Hawaii.

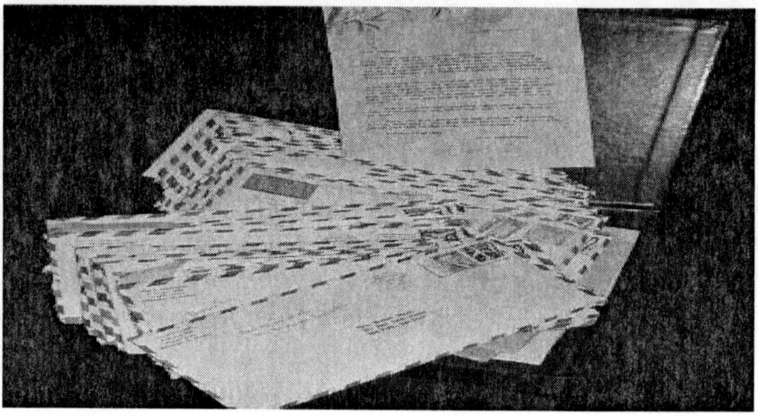

Finally it had come! The acceptance letter! I was Joel Goldsmith's student, and I was committed "to going the whole way"!

The next morning I mailed my registration form. I wanted to be included in the Class to be conducted at the Mission Inn in California, two months hence.

## Chapter 7

### Meeting Joel

**We are all bound toward a promise.**
**Who will show me the way?**

The letter was postmarked Redondo Beach, California, January 29, 1962. It was leap year, and as I opened the envelope my heart was leaping with joy! Joel Goldsmith had accepted me as a student and I was on my way to join others in one of his "closed" classes scheduled 5 weeks hence, in California.

The letter read, "*Dear Mrs. Stark,*

*I have made your room reservation for Joel's class at the Mission Inn (March 10-18) as you requested. Have also listed your name for the class. So happy to know you will be with us to share such a wonderful experience as all of Joel's classes are. When you send your tuition fee make the check payable to Joel S. Goldsmith & send to me.*

*My blessings, Aloha – Carmen Sawtelle*

*PS The Mission Inn will send confirmation of your room reservation. C.S."*

Included with the letter was a picture postcard.

I had just over 5 weeks to plan my journey to California, and my mind raced to put the priorities in order. On the list of things to do were arranging transportation, from Manhattan to the airport, making a reservation on the transcontinental flight, selecting a suitable and attractive wardrobe, and making certain Morty's needs were attended to during my one week absence. I had never been apart from him before except when he traveled from our Manhattan home on business.

At the top of my list of things to do was, "make a reservation from New York to Los Angeles." I telephoned a local travel agent to enquire about non-stop flights, asking if there were flights from LaGuardia Airport, the closest airport to where we lived. The agent advised me that all non-stop flights departed from

Idlewild International Airport in Queens. I was informed that there were several airlines from which I could choose. She recommended Pan American World Airways. The agent informed me that, "the flight from the east to the west coast would be a long and tiring one, with a three-hour time difference." That is when I decided that I should plan my arrival the day prior to the scheduled classes. It would give me the opportunity to adjust to both the time and climate change while getting acclimated with my new surroundings. My list also included arranging transportation from the Los Angeles Airport to the Mission Inn. Perhaps Morty had some suggestions.

I knew that I needed to allocate several hours a day preparing mentally and spiritually for what would be emotionally and intellectually challenging classes. I needed to spend many hours over the next weeks meditating on Joel's writings and listening to his audiotapes. I underline "study and meditate" on my list.

But there were other fretting problems that concerned me. I had faced none of them before. I would be away from Morty, on my own, for the first time ever. He was my "comfort and my strength". There was also the question of how to tell my mother about my travel plans and my promise to her that I would never enter the doors of an airplane. Then there was also my lifelong phobia of becoming nauseated, a certainty if I would be sitting on an airplane for more than five hours!

Morty and I spoke about our absence from each other at dinner that night. He reminded me of earlier absences when he had traveled internationally and domestically on business. During those times when we were apart, we wrote letters, some mailed to each other and others kept to be read when we next were together. He assured me that he would call me every day.

My fear of being airsick was another matter! I was sitting alone at home the next morning not knowing how I might control my fear. I said to God, "You have to help me overcome this!" At the same moment came the unmistakable reply from God, "**I** won't let you get sick!" There was no mistaking His assurance and I indeed recognized this as the still, small voice of God. Should I have been surprised that God would become involved and concerned about what most would probably call a trivial matter? I thought not, after all His promise in the Bible says, "Lo, I am with you always".

Mother's fear of my flying would be the most difficult concern to overcome.

Mother had warned me against flying for many years. I was certain that the only way to broach the subject was by visiting her personally, certainly not over the telephone. I taxied to her home to break the news.

When I announced my intentions to travel to Los Angeles aboard Pan American World Airways, she became more emphatic than ever on the subject of my flying. She reminded me of the newspaper articles detailing the many clippers that had been lost. There were a string of them, actually, in the years prior to my planned flight; seven were lost in the 1950s alone. Another had been lost in 1961 in Germany, just months before my scheduled Pan Am flight.

Mother was not a religious person and could not relate to my argument that I was in the hands of the Infinite. whether airborne or not. I loved mother very much and was anxious for her to understand where I stood in my spiritual quest. However, having tried so many times through the years to speak with her of spiritual matters I felt it hopeless to continue. I would simply have to put her future in the hands of an all- knowing and all-powerful God through my prayers. Mother walked me to the door and we hugged. She said, "Be safe." In my heart I knew I would be. It was time for me to move to the next level.

While I was preparing for my pilgrim journey, I often thought of how the Spirit had led me steadily, step by step. In our earthly life, even though fully committed to God, it is never a matter of a final arrival, but rather, a continual pursuit of striving ever higher. To go forward, to move upward, and to reach the next level is a steady conscious commitment to living in the Infinite. It is saying to God, "Just as I am, I consecrate myself to Thee." This is a growing process. We come humbly before our God and ask for enlightenment so that we might continue to walk in the Spirit.

To enter into a deeper consecration, I would require a deeper search. For me, the deeper search would come about by studying and meditating at the feet of the master, Joel Goldsmith. I was thrilled that I had been accepted as a private student. Joel's acceptance of me as a student was a Divine and mystical confirmation.

A story often told by Joel was a fable about an old sage. The story was really an analogy of my own spiritual discernment, direction and experience. I believed intuitively that Joel saw in the parable my own development and that is what prompted him to accept me:

An old sage had lived a full, and in his mind, a good and honorable life. He had been kind and shared his considerable wisdom with all who came to him seeking advice. After many years of helping any and all that came to him, the sage felt the time had come for him to leave his earthly role and enjoy eternity in heaven.

The sage stood at the door to heaven and knocked. God responded to his knock and said, "Who is it?"

"It is I," replied the sage. After a moment of silence God said, "Sorry, We have no room for you. Come back some other time." The sage, rebuffed by God, returned to earth pondering his predicament. After two years he thought it time to again seek entry into heaven.

The sage stood again at the now familiar door and knocked. God's response was the same "Who is it?"

"It is I," replied the sage. There was a moment of silence and God said, "Sorry, We have no room for you. Come back some other time!"

The sage returned to earth and once again took up his duties. Three years later he again returned to heaven's gates and knocked. "Who is it," asked God. "It is You," he replied. God swung wide the gates and said, "Welcome home."

I understood the story long before it became my own! I knew that studying with Joel would move me further in making the YOU experience a constant spiritual reality in my life. It is the Holy Spirit who desires our growth and He will certainly accomplish our salvation to the end so that we will also hear the "Welcome home!"

Recently a friend shared the words of a song written by an Australian. He was heir to a great corporate fortune, but forsook the wealth to instead serve as a Salvation Army officer, taking the message of a heavenly welcome to the downtrodden.

O how I'd like to see his face,
My Lord beholding!
Oh how I'd like to take my place
His arms enfolding!
Someday I'll cross old Jordan's tide,

Some day the gates will open wide.
Then I shall at his feet abide,
My Lord beholding.

Some day I'll see his blessed face,
Some day I'll see his blessed face,
I'll hear the music of his voice,
Some glad, sweet day.

Arthur Smith Arnott

My clothes and other essentials were packed the night before my scheduled departure on March 10. Morty was careful to remind, more than once, that we needed to allow two hours for the drive to Idlewild Airport. We arrived with sufficient time for us to enjoy a morning cup of coffee in the Golden Door Restaurant. First though, we went to the newly constructed Pan Am departure terminal where I checked in and had my bags tagged to LAX. Morty had made arrangements for me to be met at the Los Angeles International Airport by a business associate. I was to look for a man wearing a red Carnation on his lapel.

We said farewell at the gate. I was ushered onboard and the stewardess escorted me to my seat. A gentleman, obviously a businessman, was comfortably seated and blocked my access to my window seat. Rather than standing up to allow me to pass to my seat, he swung his knees to the side, while clutching his briefcase, allowing me only the slightest entry. I squeezed past him to my seat. A few minutes later we were asked to fasten our seat belts, relax, and expect the flight to Los Angeles to be just over five hours.

The roar of the jet engines and the lurch of the giant Boeing 707 was completely unexpected. After all, this was my first flight. The plane lumbered slowly at first – I looked out of the small window wondering how the mass of riveted steel could possibly become airborne and stay that way! The large wings buoyed on the air under them as we gained speed, and then – the ground began to drop below as we climbed steadily over Long Island Sound. The plane banked and I saw ships below becoming smaller and smaller on the cresting waves. My mind went back to my first journey over the sound, aboard the French Line's De Grasse, four decades earlier. I could see the skyline of Queens and Manhattan in the distance on my right. I recall thinking that nothing much had changed in those 40 years. The only major new construction under way was the Verrazano Bridge that I viewed below. It would take another two years to complete. A minute later the Captain announced that we were passing Newark Airport as we continued our climb.

The "No Smoking" sign and "Fasten Seat Belt" signs were turned off when we were about ten minutes into our flight. As we climbed through 10,000 feet, we were offered champagne and a mix of other drinks prior to lunch being served

The Captain exited the cockpit and came to greet us. He informed us that we were now flying over Pennsylvania. It was all very exciting. However, my phobia about flying suddenly became very real. I began to feel quite sick. I had a phobia about being nauseated all my life. I began to panic… of all the inopportune times for this malady to strike! I closed my eyes and began wondering if I should go to the airplane's tiny restroom or stay in my seat and try to fight off my queasiness. I opened my eyes, wondering if perhaps I should make a run for it. On my left, I noticed again the open briefcase and the thought of using the briefcase as a sick bag brought a momentary giggle. However, I'm certain if I resorted to using the briefcase it would not have been amusing to my fellow passenger.

Joel's book, *The Infinite Way*, was tucked into the seat pocket directly in front of me along with magazines and a sick bag. I quickly searched for the book, finding the air sickness-bag along with it. I recall the look of despair on my seatmate as I removed the bag and book. No doubt that my fellow passenger was intently watching, hoping that my activities were directed to the book and not to the airsickness-bag!

The book fell open in my hands and I became enveloped in a beautiful peace. It was a "peace that passes understanding." To me, this was a miracle, and only later did I connect it with God's assurance that had come to me while seated at home in my living room chair.

I waited a few minutes before going to the restroom where I looked in the mirror. I suppose I should have been surprised, but I really was not. There was an aura about the mirrored reflection. I returned to the cabin, took a different seat with no one next to me, and the remainder of the journey was absolutely serene. I felt as though God and I were pilot and co-pilot, as though we were in control of the entire airplane.

I glanced at the page that had opened in Joel's book and the words reminded me that we are living between two worlds, the material world whereby one assigns powers to persons, things and conditions, and the world of spiritual awareness. Joel's words reminded me to believe that there is something greater than those external powers. The words from one of his lectures came to me, where he reminded the listeners that we can elect to faze out our human reaction. We can draw ourselves into a higher consciousness in order that no influence "out in the air" can have power over us. I had studied and begun to assimilate this truth in practice. It was becoming a part of me. This pilgrimage would lead me farther.

On arrival in Los Angeles, I disembarked the aircraft and entered the terminal building. The very first person I noticed, standing to the side of the check-in counter, was a distinguished looking gentleman wearing a bright red carnation. He introduced himself and his lovely wife as we walked to the luggage claim area.

As we departed the terminal building walking towards the parking lot, I suddenly felt a coldness overcome my spirit, something I had not sensed before – a deep sense of loneliness. The warmth and kindness of these two newfound friends did nothing to dissuade or offset my sudden homesickness. I longed to be close to Morty. As we drove along the busy freeway, I felt the sudden urge to cry, and wondered if I could ask them to turn the car around and get me back to the airport so that I could catch the next flight to New York. I still had Joel's book near me in my carry-on flight bag. I was too embarrassed to remove it from the bag, so I clutched the bag. Again my mind became settled, and I found at least for the moment, an inward peace.

We arrived at the Mission Inn and I was struck by its magnificence and grandeur. I had received a postcard with a picture of the hotel. However, prior to receiving it, I had pictured myself as a spiritual novice on a pilgrimage traveling to a place of retreat, a rustic camp or convent in a setting far from human contact. I still had much to learn about where God resides.

My friends asked if I would like them to stay while I got settled. I assured them that I was fine and thanked them for their kindness.

I checked in at the front desk as a bellhop stood nearby waiting to carry my bags and show me to my room. I was handed my room key, and with it a small packet containing a welcome letter to the "closed" class, and general information about Riverside, the city where I would reside for the next eight days.

I entered my room, tossed my carry-on bag on the bed and tipped the bellhop as I closed the door behind him. I was again overcome by my emotions. I felt desperately alone – thoughts flooded me, reminding me that I was thousands of miles from my secure world- my home and Morty. I desperately needed to cry! The tears were on their way when I noticed that Joel's book had spilled from my bag and was lying beside the flight bag. Once again, the peace returned miraculously. I decided that my cry could wait until I had showered. I had already been on my feet for more than 17 hours, traveled almost 3000 miles, and what I really needed was a refreshing shower. It was almost 10:00 pm. EST.

Following my shower, I reset my watch to the local Pacific Time and noted that it was dinnertime. I decided that the "cry" my emotions so desperately demanded could wait until after dinner. I went downstairs to the main dining room and was escorted to a table by a most attentive waiter.

I was dressed in my finest raiment to give myself confidence. God came through again by sending me the most adorable waiter who kept me happy all through dinner. I enjoyed his attentiveness and sense of humor -- they must have been God's welcome gifts.

With dinner completed, I returned to my room and looked out the large picture window. Spotlights set at the trunks of the many palm trees illuminated the landscaped grounds of the Mission Inn. It was an extraordinarily beautiful sight. The colors danced through the fringed palm curtain set below me. The loneliness and sadness had dissipated – I was happy to be here.

It had been a long and tiring day. By now I had been on my feet almost 20 hours. Sleep came quickly, and I dreamt that *I was walking among the illumined palm trees dressed in a fur coat, sensing that I was somehow protected by the Infinite.* The coat symbolized protection, everlasting protection. It was God honoring me because I had dared to do this. I had made the right decision and I would be rewarded for it by eternal protection.

I was not yet adjusted to the time difference between New York and California, so I had awakened quite early. I was determined to make the most of my time, so I rose and showered. I was one of very few guests at that early hour in the dining room. It was my first full day at the Mission Inn, and I wanted to allow plenty of time to become acquainted with its surroundings as well as to make a short excursion to the center of Riverside. I looked out and saw the palm trees, and in the distance the beauty of the California mountain ranges. I was truly happy that I was there.

I took the elevator to the ground floor, taking with me the packet of information that been left for me by the organizers of Joel's classes when I checked in last night. I had looked at the packet only briefly and decided to read it at my breakfast table. The packet contained the schedule of classes, a small map of Riverside, and a bus schedule indicating regular service from a nearby bus stop.

I decided to venture out. I asked the concierge where the bus stop was located and he pointed me to the street and said, “You’ll find the stop just a few minutes away, up the street. But where are you headed?” he added. I told him I had a few hours of free time and wanted to go to the center of town. He chuckled and said that I would be much more comfortable in a taxi. I replied that I needed a walk and with the hour being so early, I could well take my time getting downtown. I found the bus stop and waited only a few minutes before the RTA bus arrived. It was filled with early morning commuters headed for the center of Riverside. It was a beautiful ride along a boulevard with a median overflowing with red roses. I remarked about the beauty of the median strip, and the person seated next to me informed me that the street was eight miles long, running from the center of town to the university.

I spent the next few hours window shopping and had lunch before returning to the hotel. My discomfort of the day before had vanished completely. My spirit was bright and ready to absorb all that the classes would offer. But before that, I would make an excursion to the beach the next morning.

# Chapter 8

## Journey into Freedom

*"For my thoughts are not your thoughts, neither are your ways my ways," declares the LORD. "As the heavens are higher than the earth, so are my ways higher than your ways and my thoughts than your thoughts."*
*Isaiah 55: 8-9*

With breakfast completed I returned to my room to seek God's leading for my new day through my morning devotions. Isaiah's words had been on my mind for several days. I sensed that God wanted to reveal a new direction for my life. God was leading me to discover more deeply His desire for me to receive His spirit in and through me. A friend had shared a quote he heard at a seminar focusing on becoming more God-like, "You become what you think about most of the time". As I pondered the quote I prayed that this was the day He would open my heart to behold more of His spirit and the freedom in the Spirit.

Many people who come to a religious faith, a spiritual awakening, admit that the greatest hindrance in moving into a deeper relationship and commitment with the Infinite is the demand by Him that we deny "the self". The problem in doing so lies in our desire to be in total control of life's circumstances rather than to give control over to God. Comfortable in our setting and sufficient unto ourselves we give God a little space in our life rather than giving ourselves over completely to His planned place for our life. No doubt some of our reluctance stems from the uncertainty about what God might demand of us. What does the Spirit ask?

God asks that we empty ourselves before Him in order that He fill us. God asks that we surrender our spirit fully to His divine nature. Too often we seek to define God in accordance with our own plans, perceptions, and purpose, rather than "letting go" to be free in His spirit. We want the God who will give us what we desire rather than the God who asks us to trust His leading. We hide and deafen our ears to His admonition, "My ways are higher than your ways".

We see God as a God who wants to control rather than a God who wants to lead us in order to set us free. Into that mindset comes God's gentle words, "My thoughts are not yours. Your ways are not mine."

For the last several months God had spoken to my heart and in so doing helped me in examining more closely my devotion – my spirit's openness to be fully consumed by His spirit. Joel Goldsmith's teaching had brought great insight; yet, my spirit was yearning for a fuller understanding of "freedom of the spirit". Was it a question of my having to give more of myself? Or was I to wait for God to bestow more of His grace on me in order for me to understand His purpose and plan? Simply put, God never limits the grace He bestows; rather, we close ourselves off thereby limiting His ability to pour out more of Himself.

At breakfast I had read in the local paper a story about an American tourist in Paris, who purchased an inexpensive amber necklace in a trinket shop, and was shocked when he had to pay quite a high duty on it to clear customs on arrival in New York. This aroused his curiosity, so he had it appraised. After looking at the object under a magnifying glass, the jeweler said, “I’ll give you $25,000 for it.” Greatly surprised, the man decided to have another expert examine it. When he did, he was offered $10,000 more. “What do you see that’s so valuable about this old necklace?” asked the astonished man. “Look through this glass,” replied the jeweler. There before his eyes was an inscription: “From Napoleon Bonaparte to Josephine.” The value of the necklace came from its identification with the famous giver of the gift.

I thought about that story as I continued my devotions thanking God for the many gifts He continually showered on me, more than can be numbered. I knew I couldn’t possibly count them all, I none-the-less reflected on His goodness. It was then that I realized that God had withheld nothing from me. My sense of inadequacy in giving myself more fully lay in my own decision, in my withholding a part of me from Him.

I realized that God’s greatest gift to me was not a thing, not pardon, peace, purity… It was Himself. I became aware that God had inscribed on my soul, my very being, “From God to Evelyn I give My divine nature”.

We are made partakers of the Divine and we receive the life of God in our soul. Not only do we become His but He becomes ours, forever, and ever. While all His gifts to us are wonderful and expressive of His love, greater than all the gifts is the Giver. He consumes and dwells in us who are His children.

His gifts are of every kind and to meet every need, needs of the spirit, the mind and the body – gifts of necessity and gifts of pure luxury. Most especially I thanked my gracious God for giving me His divine nature as I silently recited my words of thanksgiving. My heart sang a song of joy knowing that His divine nature was my nature.

As I looked out of my hotel room window I saw the California mountain ranges in the far distance. Truly this was a gift of pure luxury. The mountain peaks were bathed with the early morning sun. A low mist reflected the sun's rays upward to unfold the beauty of the hills. The sun's rays cascaded down along the valleys bouncing from shadow to shadow as the morning mist dissipated. The gleaming rays ran the full length from the mountain peaks through the valleys to finally stream through the window and spill over me. It was God saying' Good morning Evelyn, this day is a gift from Me!"

I had a full 10 hours of free time until I was to meet with my fellow students in Joel Goldsmith's "closed class". The Mission Inn was located in an area called the Inland Empire. In the distance to the west was the San Bernardino National Forest. I had the choice to visit nearby places of interest or the mountains, but my mind went westward, to the Pacific Ocean. On our final approach to Los Angeles International Airport yesterday, we had flown over many of the famous California beaches. I had read about them, seen them on TV and in movies. The ocean was my first choice.

The concierge hailed a taxi for me. I wasn't certain which beach to visit so I asked the taxi driver what he might recommend. He asked me what I was interested in seeing. It was still early spring and my interest was simply to take a walk along a beach, relax and to get some fresh air. I told him though that I would be interested to see surfboard riders, something I had only seen in movies. He suggested, "Long Beach, San Pedro, Redondo, and El Porto, where an underwater canyon creates a challenging swell. The Redondo El Porto seems to be the favorite, as you can tell by the size of the crowds." He told me that I had come at just the right season because the waves were the highest and most challenging in the winter and spring months.

He dropped me off near the pier and pointed out some of the popular eating establishments in case I wanted to break for lunch. We agreed that he'd pick me up at 4:00 pm for the return ride to the Mission Inn.

The day was wonderful… the sea air, the many joggers, lunch at an outdoor café, and the surfers bobbing on their boards waiting for the "perfect wave'. It was all so vibrant and alive! I was especially interested in the grace of the surfers. They would wait for several minutes for just the right wave before making their turn to shore, paddling furiously as they effortlessly hauled themselves to their feet guiding their board so skillfully in and out of the crescents. There seemed to be such a special kind of freedom in their pursuit. It was as though they were free to fly across the waves!

But, around 2:00 o'clock something very strange happened… It suddenly occurred to me that the waves were thwarted from coming close to shore. The surfers sat on their boards waiting to be carried on the waves, but the waves broke long before coming near shore. The surfers finally gave up waiting and paddled to shore, packed their gear, and departed. It seemed very strange to me.

I asked one of the many persons strolling the beach what had so suddenly ended the surfers' quest. He explained to me that unseen by the eye, just below the surface there lies a sandbar. As the tide moves out the sandbar swallows up the crashing waves turning them into rushing foam. He said that when the tide returns however, the full force of the ocean would once again be there to lift the surfers' board above the sandbar, free again to skim the waves the full length to shore.

As the phenomenon of the waves was explained it was a revelation to me. I understood that God was telling me that I too, for many years, had allowed a hindrance, a sandbar of sorts, to halt the full flow of His blessings into my life. It wasn't something I was conscious of, but through this little excursion of mine God reminded me of an ancient truth. He who is free is free indeed – free in every sense of the word. Freedom in the Spirit means giving over completely, giving over every part of oneself. Frankly, I thought I had done so, but there were those times when in desperation I prayed like David in Psalm 27:9 pleading, "Do not hide your face from me, do not turn your servant away in anger; you have been my helper. Do not reject me or forsake me, O God my Savior."

As I reflected on those times when I had felt so utterly alone, separated from God by the "sandbar", I realized that it was at those periods in my life when I withheld myself from Him. It was those times when I sought to live "free" of Him in my own strength. Vanity had been guiding me, materialism ruled. I had been seeking to live by my own resources. Instead, I had to constantly strive to move from living on a horizontal plane, that plane where I am in control, to a vertical plane, coming to God with a purity of motive, focusing on Him. The vertical plane is the divine realm where God rewards the seeker by welcoming us into a mature spiritual experience.

In my morning devotions back in my hotel room I had sensed anew God's love for me, that same invitation He had extended me many years ago, to come fully into His freedom; to abide there. My visit to the beach was God's stark reminder of both that promise and His clear message of the reason for any separation from Him. I knew that if there was ever a separation or absence from His spirit, I was responsible. I reminded myself of His precious promise to me, "I will never leave you or forsake you".

As I was driven back to the Mission Inn I thought about my Enlightenment – my Freedom and prayed a silent prayer of thanksgiving.

The freedom I had found within had grown steadily through the years and had come about through my studying and meditating. I matured year by year to learn that freedom came through making an ever-stronger commitment to the Infinite. As paradoxical as it may sound, spiritual freedom comes through yielding oneself in love and joy to the Eternal. It is the complete surrender of my will to God's will. Then I must go on giving myself, day by day acknowledging His presence being lived through me and as me

The writings of the Jewish philosopher Martin Buber helped me to understand this surrender into freedom. He taught me through explaining the meaning of the pronoun Thou. The I had to be emptied and filled with the Thou. Thou had to replace my ego for me to become free. I, Evelyn, was simply a channel of awareness through which God could express Himself.

**To My Child**

**Oh you poor dear sweet child who was me,**
**When you only could hear, touch and see**
**With your physical senses**
**Living in the parenthesis**
**Not knowing your identity.**

**How different is everything now**
**Awake to your I and your Thou**
**Enlightened and free**
**Dearest child that was me**
**Go forward for now you know how.**

Evelyn Brill Stark

## Chapter 9

### Foreboding

**Pray as though everything depended on God; WORK as though everything depended on you. –**
St. Augustine

Before leaving New York for California I had two dreams that seemed harbingers of what was to come. The first lifted my spirit while the second brought a sense of foreboding.

The first dream was about a beautiful pink coat that I saw in the window of Elizabeth Arden's in Manhattan. I did not know the significance of the color, but can only share that it was the most beautiful coat I had ever seen. A few days after I dreamt of that coat, I passed the Arden's store on Madison Avenue. Naturally, I looked at the storefront to see if there was a pink coat in the window. I was not surprised to see that there was no such coat, yet my intuition told me I really ought to step in and ask if they had a coat like the one in my dream.

I spoke to a sales person and shared that I thought I had seen a pink coat in the window some days earlier. To my great surprise the sales clerk said, "We had a coat like that in the window last autumn as a part of the fall collection. It is now on sale at 50% off, as we will have a whole new collection next autumn." With that said she led me to a rack of clothing on sale and there was the coat, exactly as I had seen it in my dream. I mused out loud, "I'll take it!" I bought the coat on the spot.

What possible connection could that dream have with my going to California to attend the Goldsmith class? In my dream the coat was the color of love. Was this a premonition of what I would experience in those classes? I was soon to enter a new spiritual plane. Could this be an outward symbol of security, of love?

In the other dream I saw myself in a large maze surrounded on all sides by a very high hedge, too high to see over. I sought every possible exit only to become more and more lost and confused. No matter which direction I turned everything looked the same. I backtracked hoping I could find the entrance, but to no avail. It was not clear to me what the dream signified when I woke, but I sensed that somehow I was going to get lost in California. Sure enough that too happened!

In my excitement to see the beautiful Pacific Ocean beaches on my first full day in California, I had left my taxi without giving much attention to landmarks, to where my taxi driver was going to pick me up five hours later. Instead, I had focused on the many sights and sounds I experienced during my walk along the beach. When it came time to look for my ride back to the Mission Inn, I realized that I had no idea where I was. I didn't even know in what direction to turn.

I asked a gentleman strolling near me if he could help me find my way. After several minutes of trying to recall any significant landmarks to identify where the taxi had dropped me, I mentioned that there was a roundabout of some kind. Some of the cars circled as though waiting for someone to alight before setting off. Other cars stopped briefly as passengers were dropped off, most of them walking down a few steps to the beach. The man knew immediately which part of the beach I was describing. He walked with me about a half mile before pointing me towards the stairs. I climbed the steps and there was the taxi, having waited for more than a half hour.

During the next few days the dream's symbolic significance became clear. I was a newcomer to the "closed" class. Much of the conscious spirituality experienced by the others in my class became evident in the very first session. Spiritually, I had come to the point where I needed direction to lead me further. I was unfocussed, unable to find my way on my own.

I had always known that I possessed preternatural tendencies concerning spiritual matters but lacked direction.

As I made my way to the assigned meeting room where the first class would be conducted, the only one open to the public, I looked forward to what God was going to bring me next. I was wearing my new pink coat.

The lecture was conducted in a large room filled to capacity. I put my nametag on my lapel and found a place to sit. Although open to the general public, many in the room appeared well acquainted. There appeared to be a great spirit of camaraderie. I did not know anyone there, so I simply remained in my seat waiting for Joel to appear. All of a sudden the noise of the crowd became a hush of anticipation, and Joel stepped into the room wearing one of his familiar string bow ties and went to the lectern. There was an otherworldly, a celestial radiance about him as he fixed an arresting stare on us all.

In his introductory lecture Joel said, “God is the mind of me, the life, the Soul, the Spirit, and God is my capacity. I have access to infinite intelligence, to infinite, eternal Life. I have access to infinite supply, infinite harmony, peace, and perfection- to all of these because I have access to infinity.” And he spoke of life being meaningless without God, “…without God life is more or less accidental. One of the greatest lessons of Hebrew Scripture is, ’Except the Lord build the house, they labor in vain that build it.’ “Except we take God into our intimate lives, the final outcome is not going to be harmonious, successful, joyous.”

Joel continued by focusing on a basic principle of *The Infinite Way*, which is found in the word, IS. God IS, harmony IS, life IS, love IS, peace IS, joy IS, power IS, and dominion IS because God “IS”. God is infinite, omnipresent, omnipotent and omniscient. God already “IS”. I remember how powerful Joel’s message was. In particular I remember Joel speaking, as to me alone, saying, “you can never fear God once you realize God as the “I” within, because you will know then that the nature of God is as light touching darkness.”

I had studied and meditated on this reality many times, but never in a group setting, a setting where everyone seemed to be in tune with the Infinite, the “I” within. God’s spirit seemed to envelop the room and everyone in it. Even though this was a lecture open to the public there was a sense of family that I had never experienced before. We were immersed in Love. Joel was the conduit of that love.

I was anxious to introduce myself to Joel following his message, but as soon as he finished, a large crowd surrounded him. I would be there for eight days and knew there would be other opportunities. Tomorrow the "closed" classes would begin and there would be a much smaller, more intimate group.

Sure enough, the next day I saw Joel at lunchtime. I introduced myself saying, "Hello, I'm Evelyn Stark." Joel was sitting at a table with three other people including his wife. Joel replied, "Oh, yes. Evelyn Stark. I know who you are. It's so good that you could join our class. You know Evelyn, I get an awful lot of mail, but I always know somehow when there's a letter from you. I always enjoy hearing from you." I was filled with unspeakable joy to learn that my teacher found my letters so special.

I was very much a loner with no one to talk to, so that morning at breakfast I went up to one of the persons wearing a nametag and said, "I'm Evelyn Stark from New York. I traveled 3000 miles to be here. I left my husband all alone. I do not know anyone here. Could you help me?" She introduced herself as Mae Shaw and immediately took my arm as she led me to a small group and said, "I'll introduce you to the inner circle". I met Virginia Stevenson, Betty Brainerd, and Jean Fugle, persons who had been a part of Joel's inner circle for many years. They all took me under their wings. From that day on we had breakfast together each morning, met in each other's rooms to share stories and spiritual insight. I liked them, and they liked me. There is a very strong bond when friendships are forged on a spiritual plane.

I had read everything ever published by Joel and many of his newsletters. I had listened to his audiotapes for years. I had more than 130 seven-inch, reel-to-reel tapes in my Goldsmith collection. But hearing the message live, in a setting with only a select group of students, was a very unique spiritual experience. The message was alive and more relevant than ever before. It was the master speaking to his disciples.

I truly enjoyed the spiritual fellowship, yet I was disappointed that Joel Goldsmith had not invited me to a private audience with him. After all, that was a key reason for my having traveled cross-country! So finally, two days prior to the course ending I decided I had to confront Joel. I was seated in the dining room alone, at lunchtime, when Joel came over to my table to say hello. After that first meeting at lunch earlier in the week, Joel had been very friendly, always acknowledging me as we saw or passed each other. He would wave or smile at me. I said to Joel, "I haven't had an interview with you, yet I came 3,000 miles from New York to see you. I know you have many appointments and I would appreciate one of them being with me!"

Joel looked at me a bit quizzically, answering apologetically, "Evelyn, I'm sorry but I don't do my own scheduling, it's done for me. I will see that it's straightened out right away!"

When I returned to my room later that afternoon there was a message waiting for me.

"Mr. Joel Goldsmith invites you to a private meeting tomorrow afternoon at 4:00 p.m. in his office."

My mind raced as I thought about the many spiritual concerns I had – the questions I would ask. I also thought to myself, what might he ask?

I went to his office the next afternoon. Joel rose from behind his desk as I entered and invited me to be seated. I felt especially privileged that he would see me privately, particularly in view of the large retinue of devotees no doubt seeking a similar personal interview.

Before Joel could say a word I said to him, "I have been true to you for eight years." I could see a faint blush come to his cheeks as he raised his furrowed brows quizzically. I continued, "I have been listening to your tapes alone in my study because I wanted to get the message absorbed in my consciousness." I also shared how very special I felt because he had finally accepted me as a private student.

Joel reminded me of the unique and solemn relationship between teacher and student, what he had written to me some months earlier. He then asked if I had experienced any particular insights recently – had I received any special messages.

I shared with him the details of my two dreams. He showed little interest in them and dismissed them saying we would talk about dreams at another time.

Then I told him about the ethereal message emanating from a voice that came from the living room when I was seated in a chair at home in New York, when I was frightened of becoming nauseated.

I joked animatedly that, "I didn't care if the whole plane crashed as long as I didn't get airsick." He laughed. I continued, "A still small voice had said, I won't let you get sick." I asked if Joel thought that it was God speaking to me, and he immediately replied with an emphatic "yes". Joel continued, "And did you get sick?" I replied, "No, but had the flight been another five minutes longer I wouldn't have guaranteed anything." Joel laughed heartily at that.

Joel spoke for some minutes about my need to recognize the very unique contrast between personal friendships, like those formed with my newfound friends, and one formed between a student and teacher. A most enlightening part of our private meeting was when he elaborated by saying that I may have gathered the impression that there are "beginning" students and "advanced" students. He said that I must begin to break down that impression immediately. "As far as God is concerned, it makes no difference whether you are coming to Him for the first time or you have been doing so for a lifetime."

Joel explained that God's sufficiency is found in the Grace He bestows on every seeker of Truth, "Meeting those needs where you are now and at this moment. Once you realize this you'll make rapid progress through your studies and meditations. In this moment God's Grace is your sufficiency and so it will continue to be."

Joel concluded our session by again emphasizing the relationship between a spiritual teacher and a student being a sacred one. It was a most inspiring meeting.

The days that followed were ones of meditation and fellowship. My mornings began with private devotions followed by breakfast with my friends. During the day we would meet for discussion and meditation. Joel's words about there being no "beginning" or "advanced" students were a revelation to me. On my arrival I had naively assumed that students who had been disciples of Joel for many years somehow had unique access to the Infinite. I realized how right Joel was in instructing us on God's gift of spiritual insight.

Spiritual insight has little value unless it is applied in a practical way in one's search for a deeper relationship with the Infinite. It is poured out of God's plentiful bounty by grace on us, no matter whether a novice seeker of the Infinite, or a disciple of many years. The key is to be mindful of the Giver and our responsibility to respond.

Joel's admonition was the simple truth found in the words of Jesus, "Suffer the children to come unto me." That is how I came, as the seeking child. That is how we all must come. Come believing, come expecting. I felt more and more immersed in a spirit of divine Love.

Another, and perhaps the most significant lesson of the week for me, was learning the simple significance of prayer.

In Joel's lecture on prayer he said,

> "Prayer is an attitude that is built upon our understanding of truth. In other words, if from morning to night and from night until morning I am recognizing you (other persons) as the instrument, the very presence of God, that place where God shines through, I am praying without ceasing (the result of that recognition). If I behold discord of any kind emanating from you, I am still living my life of prayer by my recognition that this is not you; this is merely the carnal mind finding an outlet temporarily. By impersonalising I help to destroy it. I bless you as much as I bless you when I recognize that you are the presence of God. I would not be in prayer if I said you are good or you are spiritual. I would not be blessing you if I said you are sick or you are sinful. But I am living a consistent life of prayer without ceasing when I am beholding you as a child of God-the instrument of God.
>
> Prayer is bestowing… Prayer is not an instrument whereby we get, prayer is an instrument whereby we give, share, bestow, recognize, bless. Prayer is a benediction, a blessing…
>
> Prayer must be an outlet for the Christ, which does not judge or condemn, which is forever saying, "I will forgive thee seventy times seven. Put up thy swords."

I learned and understood that prayer is a way of life – it is the ever-present reminder that we are grounded in Truth, living and moving consciously to love our fellow man. In prayer I am acknowledging thanksgiving to the source of all Truth.

Joel said in his closed class, "The life of prayer is a life of blessing. Before coming to a life of prayer you must have to be touched in your heart. Once you're touched in your heart there's no reason to do anything for your own sake. Your own major problems are finished." My heart had been touched countless times and I began and ended each day with prayer. Yet I hadn't understood fully the nature or form of prayer. He added, "Prayer is bestowing outwardly… you yourself begin to be a blessing… the Christ flows through you to bless others. He quoted Ralph Waldo Emerson, and said, " Your mind is an inlet and an outlet from the mind of God".

It should have been no surprise then that God's revelation came to me. It was the truth Joel had been sharing all week. That is why I felt such a strong presence of Truth when fellowshipping with my friends or in class. We were abiding, living in the consciousness of the Infinite.

The California visit came to an end all too fast. I met with my friends for a late lunch that last day, no longer just friends any more, but a spiritual family. We spoke about upcoming lectures in New York and Chicago, and vowed we would all come together again in a few weeks. We also agreed to meet each other in meditation.

They helped me with my bags and drove me to the airport. It was dusk and one of those balmy California evenings. A small mist was sweeping inland from the Pacific Ocean as the car pulled to the curb at the Pan American Airlines terminal. After saying farewell at the curb, I gave my bags to a skycap and went to the departure gate.

When the flight to New York lifted from the ground I could see the lights of cars below on the Pacific Highway. My new found friends were in one of the cars. It was already getting dark, but I could see the beaches stretching out beneath me. Dinner was served, and we were told a movie would soon be shown.

The flight attendant asked if I would like a pillow and blanket. She told me that with the difference in time, three hours, dawn would come quickly and maybe I would like to sleep. I told her I was too tense to sleep, "but not about the flying", I added. She wished me a pleasant flight and moved on. I looked around the cabin and noticed that most of the passengers were asleep with only a few watching the movie.

I reflected on the words of the flight attendant and thought of the spiritual dawning that had occurred in my life. I looked out of my little window, and my thoughts were running deep. The silence around me was complete. God and I alone watched as the light of a new day brought the dawning. Yet I also felt the presence of Joel and the friends I had bonded with spiritually at the Mission Inn. It was as though we were in a circle, meditating, sending prayers to each other and to the Infinite. The closeness of Joel was indescribable. Could it be possible? I decided that I would write to Joel about it once back in New York. I had a vision that all of them pleaded with me to become a "messenger" of the Infinite Way…

It was in the knowledge of this revelation, in God's presence, that I declared on my return flight to New York that I would prayerfully seek ways to share the Infinite Way message in every way possible. Compromises had too often controlled my direction in insidious ways. Now I wanted to align myself completely with God's purpose. I had to reconsider my life and how I was living it. Although my life in New York could not have been described as being complex, it none-the-less brought distractions, robbing me of a closer communion with God and His purpose for my life.

I recalled Joel's words in one of his Mission Inn lectures and referred to my hand written notes, "The life of prayer knows no fear, not even the fear of death. When fear is totally gone we know that we're fully developed in the life of prayer."

That was my experience. I gave no thought to my lifelong reluctance to fly, my fear of becoming airsick. God had removed all fear from me. I was in perfect peace as we jetted our way back to New York. The peace I sensed was one I had experienced from time-to-time. Now, however it remained with me. I was surrounded and lifted up by it. I had presented my needs to God and He had answered me. God knew my condition and knew what was best for me.

The scriptures tell us,

**Find rest, O my soul, in God alone;**
**my hope comes from him.**
**He alone is my rock and my salvation;**
**he is my fortress, I will never be shaken.**
Psalm 62, 5-6

I dozed briefly during the flight, unable to sleep due to my excitement, knowing Morty would be waiting for me. The flight attendant made the announcement, "Please fasten your seat belt in preparation for our landing at Idlewild Airport and extinguish all smoking material." Below me was Long Island Sound, glistening in the early morning sun. Finally, my Pan Am flight landed and we taxied to our gate. As soon as I walked up the jet way I saw two, tall handsome men waiting expectantly to the side of the crowd, Morty and my son Henry. It was a wonderful homecoming present! I do not remember if I ran to them or if angels carried me. Even though I had been in the air for more than six hours I felt absolutely aglow, physically and spiritually.

Morty took my flight bag as we walked toward the baggage claim area. It was a beautiful spring morning and no need for a coat. I was thankful for that because I no longer had my pink coat. I gave it as gift to a fellow student who had admired it in California.

## Chapter 10

### The Kingdom of God

**"Set your mind on God's kingdom and his justice before everything else, and the rest will come to you as well. So do not be anxious about tomorrow: tomorrow will look after itself…"**

The Sermon on the Mount Mathew 6:33-34

It was my first day back home in New York, and I knew my life would never be the same. I was a different person from the one who left Manhattan just a week earlier.

I returned home to find a bundle of telephone messages and mail on the kitchen table. Morty had acted as my "secretary". Meticulous notes had been recorded of the many telephone messages left for me during my absence. I riffed through the bundle and many read, "call me as soon as you get home", others, "don't forget to pick up tickets for the concert," or "a table is reserved for four at The Oak Room this Friday at noon"… I suddenly realized the "busyness" of my life. Joel had emphasized in the "closed" class that the primary activity of one seeking the Infinite was establishing and sustaining a God relationship. It was more than prioritizing one's activities, it was a matter of seeking God and His Kingdom above all else. It was not a matter of placing friends and family second; it was accepting that all these "would be added unto "me", but on a very different level. I decided at once that the harried schedule I had maintained prior to the California classes needed to be pared to more fully seek God's leading in my life.

My daily schedule was altered to allow me to meditate, pray, and study more deeply. I needed to give more time to God and less to the myriad of little things that had stolen my time from Him. I had to set aside specific times each day to push little things out of my life. I do not mean to suggest that the little things were unimportant, but rather that they easily caused fatigue and hindered my ability to give myself fully to seeking God's voice and direction. I wanted to hear Him as clearly as I did at the Mission Inn.

My visit to The Mission Inn had become what St. Paul called, "being caught up in a third heaven". St. Paul describes the experience in the opening verses of 2 Corinthians 12. Paul was in God's paradise and heard inexpressible words, words he was not permitted to share with anyone. That too had been my experience at the Mission Inn. I had been brought to the very heart of God through the revelations taught in the "closed" class. I had been enveloped in the Spirit; unspeakable joy, peace, harmony… all had swept through me. I never wanted it to leave me. It was a conscious experience. The Spirit came to each of us through personal and group meditation. God had spoken to me directly, words too holy to speak, to share.

Words will fail, none-the-less I am anxious to explain the Spirit experiences because some readers will have had a similar sense of being drawn to the Infinite, perhaps wondering if the experience was authentic. Was it of God's kingdom?

I've heard it called "crossing over", or "going to the other side", while others yet call it "another plane of consciousness". If asked to label the extraordinary experience I would call the mystical moment one in which one enters oneself, that special place where God the creator comes together with His creation. I share my definition with reluctance for fear that some will feel deprived because they have not "been there". Others may sense the expression exclusive, available and open only to some. While I believe that some are more attuned to entering the Sanctuary God offers than others, I hope that sharing my experience will help others seek it. I truly believe all can enter this plane and attain this joyous experience.

My meditations always began with an act of self-surrender. These higher spiritual encounters are never the result of a human striving and therefore never tedious or tiresome. They never come couched in a human power but are simply the result of transcendental longings.

I sought to separate myself from my outer life and enter an inward sanctuary where all of my experiences with God were stored for "remembrance". I would seek to recall those earlier experiences, those bright illuminating moments when He flooded my soul with joy. On "remembering" those experiences in prayer God would again fill me. To enter this experience one must realize that it is purely objective, outside of human experience. It is the pure work of the Holy Spirit within us enabling us to instantaneously be at one with God. It is more than just standing before God, it is recognizing the likeness of our spirit with His spirit and conforming to that likeness.

The first intuition is quite simply that time comes to a halt. One is surrounded by the vastness of the universe yet conscious of God's nearness and presence. In that experience I felt God reaching out and taking firm hold of me. I learned to attune myself to His presence in order that the experience becomes more accessible. Nature, history and the future all came together - harmony reigns in the soul with no place for discord. Past, present and future are one. Peace rules, God's peace, the peace that passes all understanding. One senses everything that has passed and all that is to come. It is the inconceivable joy of knowing that He who tossed stars into space now is One with me. It is the conscious realization that I am incorporated in all the hours that have passed since creation's very first.

I believe all persons have consciously had a mystical experience, however, if one is unaware of the source or the purpose of that experience it is often dismissed as a dream or figment of one's imagination. In reality, of course, it is God reaching down to offer harmony. I recalled the many mystical moments I had experienced and how I entered each one. Each time the experience came about by my letting go of ego and personal desires, seeking a spiritual oneness. Such longings are always outside oneself, and come at the most unexpected time and place. At times when the Spirit came in that mystical way, prior to the Mission Inn visit, it was often in a most sordid and strange place. I recall Him coming to me while waiting for our car to be brought to us in our parking garage. Another time it was while waiting for a train at Pennsylvania Station. Brilliant light would flood my spirit, and if nothing interfered with my experience, angels would dance all about me – their fluttering wings would brush against my hair.

One of the most wonderful experiences in meditating was to have an awareness of others being present. I often sensed Joel's presence along with my friends from the "closed" class. We were meditating in a kind of spiritual circle, each being aware of the other's spirit.

I wrote to Joel shortly after my return and shared this phenomenon of sensing his presence when I meditated. He wrote back to me immediately saying I should not be surprised that our spirits meet when meditating. "After all" he wrote, "we are meeting in the same source".

In addition to receiving personal correspondence from Joel I was also receiving his monthly newsletter, as were students around the world. In one of them entitled *MYSTICAL LIVING THROUGH GOD'S GRACE,* he calls that special place where we meet God, "Paradise". Here is what he wrote,

> There is no such place as a paradise. Paradise is the state of being which you are when you have learned to live in God's Grace, through God's Grace, to abide in the Word and let the Word abide in you.
>
> You will find, wherever you find groups of people who have attained God realization, you'll find peace and integrity, and health, and safety, and security. .........you have attained this inner contact with the Father.

The mystic kingdom Joel referred to is called "heavenly" and age-long" or "everlasting" in the Bible. Russell Henry Stafford in his book, *We Would See Jesus*, writes about experiencing the kingdom, "They do not make sense if we try to understand them literally, as referring respectively to the sky and to duration in time. But with a figurative reference they picturesquely point out the loftiness and the indestructible security which are implied in the idea of what we nowadays have called the eternal-that is, the transcendental, the timeless and nonspatial."

I believe Jesus intended us to understand the concept of the kingdom of God and how it exists, though perhaps beyond our ability to fully comprehend that kingdom in our consciousness. When I enter into my private meditation, I sense the harmony of God's Spirit with mine, but outside my human experience. God allows me to enter His consciousness. Because I have His spirit I am allowed to enter his kingdom.

Stafford continues, "Jesus knew the kingdom within; that is, he had throughout his ministry a sustaining experience of God's presence and power in his own life. The ground of this experience he found in the concept of the eternal kingdom, the world as it is held in the mind of God in its entirety, embracing all time and space and transcending them and perfectly fulfilling the divine intention of goodness…"

**God Morning Everyone**

**God IS and God AS!**
**What a wonderful way**
**I vision the world**
**On this glorious day.**

**The sparkling truth**
**About all that I see**
**Is that God is the table**
**And God is the tree.**

**God is the page**
**I write in this book**
**God fills the forms**
**Wherever I look.**

**God is my joy**
**And God is my sorrow**
**God is today**
**And God is tomorrow.**

**No ego deception**
**Can build up a wall**
**To hide my perception**
**God Being is All!**

Evelyn Brill Stark

In that same newsletter Joel provided instructions on how to meditate and pray.

There are, in our work, two parts to your prayer or meditation periods. The first part is that in which you

> consciously remember, declare or think, these spiritual Principles, spiritual promises, spiritual experiences of Scripture. Bring them to conscious memory, to conscious thought, dwell on them, ponder them. If possible, even contemplate them until some spiritual factor is revealed.
>
> Then comes the period of quiet for listening. It is the beginning of a meditation in which the inner ear is opened as if to hear that Voice of God, always remembering that when God utters His Voice, the earth melteth. If you receive a spiritual impulse within you, remember that the particular problem is melting, disappearing out of your life.
>
> Never forget that it is an impossibility to attain even a blink of an eye of God realization and not have some problem of human experience dissolve.
>
> And so it is that in that second part of our prayer or meditation, we are almost a vacuum, we are a transparency. We are a state of awareness as if expecting some inner unfoldment or inner feeling, or inner experience. We dare not outline what it is because we do not know the nature of God's demonstration for us….we must always have the attitude in our prayer of "Not my will be done, but Thine."

One thing to remember, no prayer must ever be advising God, or seeking in any way to influence God. Do not let yourself be trapped into those side issues. You cannot influence God. God is the same yesterday and today, and forever. If you are not receiving God's Grace, it is only because you are out of contact. Bring yourself back into contact, and the Grace will flow.

God is the all-knowing Mind. …Therefore, you must go to God a humble soul, an empty soul. "Fill me, Lord, be Thou my Grace." That's all. And when God realization takes place, you will find your needs will be fulfilled, for God is a Law of fulfillment. God is fulfillment.

Let it not be believed that mortal man is wiser than God. Let it not be believed that God will go out of His way to do for you what God is not doing for me. God's rain falls on the just and the unjust.

Although our human events take place in time and space, the terms we use for our reality, they are not the whole of reality. The action unfolds on a higher plane. They are developed and sustained in the kingdom of God. It is in that sphere, God's reality, where those who are in the spirit meet God, the Holy Spirit, and all others who are in the spirit

I always knew when Joel meditated with me. He was in Hawaii and I was in New York. I always knew that he was with me because I felt this extraordinary transcendental love. Words cannot describe what happened. How can one describe God's spirit, that which transcends the human spirit and understanding. I felt God's love was coming through Joel. When he meditated for me and with me, blockages were dissolved in my consciousness that had kept me from God. One day I heard a still small voice, God's voice. It's too sacred to put into words but I knew then I was called to serve God.

Over the next two years I traveled to many locations to again sit at the feet of the master. Each time I was inspired by a new revelation as I surrendered, seeking a glimpse of what God was asking of me. I was seeking to become His instrument.

My affection for Joel as my spiritual teacher grew steadily. God was ever more and more in my consciousness. He was present in all of my decision-making. I sought more and more ways in which I could devote myself to sharing and teaching the Infinite way.

I was committed to go ever deeper in my search for the infinite. This included regular correspondence with Joel and with my newfound friends. In the months ahead I would receive personal letters from Joel, often weekly. His messages were very personal and gracious. They included outlines for study, invitations to visit him in Hawaii, and promises to be with me in meditation and prayer.

His letters came to me from across the world. The envelopes were postmarked South Africa, Sweden, England, Austria, and of course Hawaii and mainland USA. Correspondence, addressed to me personally was arriving weekly. To think that Joel would take time to lavish such attention on a new student! Yet the more I learned to know about this teacher, the more I realized that was the kind of a man he was. I have no doubt that there were a hundred or more students writing to Joel regularly. Nor do I doubt that he gave each one the same necessary attention and spiritual direction.

I had been alerted to the coming of a spiritual teacher into my life some years prior to ever hearing his name or reading Joel's work. I regularly visited Ms. Herod, a psychic in her apartment in the Ansonia Hotel on 73rd and Broadway in New York. She told me on one of my visits, "You are going to have a spiritual counselor, this man is sending you love." I had no idea at that time who she was referring to, but now, some years later it is very clear that she was speaking about Joel Goldsmith. The spiritual teacher one "selects" will always reflect your ultimate (soul's) seeking.

God was seeking me, reaching out to me through Joel's spirit. My mystical insight was already developed and I believe it was God that led me to that Manhattan bookshop where my spirit first connected with his spirit.

Four months after my first private class in California I traveled to Chicago to again sit at the feet of the master. The lecture was conducted in the Conrad Hilton Hotel on Chicago's South Michigan Avenue. Joel stepped on stage and went to the lectern. I do not recall much of his lecture because something very strange happened. As Joel spoke, his physical presence seemed to evaporate and suddenly he was gone. I heard God's voice speaking directly to me, *"I incarnate as man."* I had grown spiritually over the past several weeks and in particular close to Joel's spirit, but yet I found this phenomenon strange and confusing. Joel had disappeared.

I tried to reason, to convince myself that it should seem natural, a type of new spiritual awakening; God had brought me to a higher plane, my God consciousness was in a new dimension. Frankly, no explanation would calm me. I shared this story with one of Joel's advanced students. Her response was, "it was an illumination."

**Optical illusion**

**I looked into a mirror**
**and saw an image there**
**An image that looked back at me**
**With strong and focused stare.**

**It broke right through my cover**
**With its piercing steely eye**
**And forced me to discover that**
**The image was a lie.**

**(The mirror was deceiving me,**
**Mirage of aging youth…**
**Reflection from a looking glass**
**Does not reveal the truth.)**

**With concentrate intensity**
**I pierced right through that eye**
**And begged "Oh Lord-please let me know**
**Thy secret. Who am I?"**

**What next befell words cannot tell**
**Not how, or when, nor why,**
**Dissolving into nothingness**
**I saw the image die.**

**A silence in me thundered:**
***Throughout thy earthly span***
***Thou art in me and I in thee***
**I INCARNATE AS MAN.**

Evelyn Brill Stark

Our correspondence continued and Joel informed in one of his letters that he would be coming to New York, staying at the Hilton Hotel. His stop over included a lecture en route from London to Hawaii. I felt compelled to send flowers to his hotel room with Morty's and my name, wishing him a warm welcome to our city. For some days prior to his arrival I felt a spiritual closeness that can't be described. I felt I needed to share that with him.

I telephoned his hotel room on the day of his arrival not knowing exactly what I would say, except perhaps, "Joel – God pushed me to call you", or simply, "Welcome to New York!"

A woman answered and I asked to speak to Joel. She asked, "Who may I say is calling?"

"Evelyn Stark", I replied. After some moments she returned to the phone and said, "Joel will speak *to* you tomorrow", and hung up. In retrospect I understood that Joel was perhaps already in bed, tired from the long flight and the change in time, five hours from that in London. I thought about her reply again, "He will speak *to* you tomorrow."

When I arrived in the lecture hall the following night the large auditorium was filled. A friend promised to save a seat for me, and fortunately I saw her wave to me from the third row as I walked in.

Joel moved to the podium and began to speak. To my surprise, Joel addressed his entire talk to me and never appeared to look at anyone else. His eyes never strayed from where I was seated. I understood then Joel's cryptic message from the evening before. When he had said "I will speak *to* you tomorrow", he had meant exactly that. I realized then that he had intuitively known why I called the day before. He was reassuring me of our spiritual union.

Following the lecture I approached Joel, waiting for the crowd around him to disperse. After some minutes I spoke to him. I simply said, "Joel you have given me everything." His fingers moved to his lips to hush me. I did not know why he wanted to hush me but remembered that on several other occasions when I attempted to share a particularly personal message, or some incident with mystical components, he would always put his fingers to his lips. It occurred to me that some things were too holy to speak about and were best left unsaid or for meditation only.

As I left him he repeated what I had heard him say in California, and also in several of his letters to me, "The relationship between a teacher and a student is very sacred. I will do anything to help you move toward the goal."

In the months and years ahead my contact with Joel continued through meditation, correspondence, and attendance in public and "closed" classes. I was totally committed to following his teaching of The Infinite Way. Our last regular contact through meditation was during the early summer of 1964. Joel was traveling in England and had arrived in London from Manchester where he conducted a "closed" class. Classes were also scheduled in London.

My meditations with Joel were somehow troubled and I couldn't understand why. I was unable to speak to him directly to seek an answer because he was in England. I sensed that our spirits were not connecting as strongly as in the past. I became unsettled and wept for several days. I sensed that his spirit was a progenitor, a pre-sentiment of sorts. Morty became very concerned about my emotional state and asked what was causing me to weep. I explained that somehow I was losing my spiritual connection with Joel, and shared that I sensed Joel would soon pass to "the other side".

During the late evening hours of June 17, 1964, I woke suddenly with a start to find Joel speaking to me. He said, "Evelyn, I am moving on." As I formulated the questions in my mind he put his fingers to his lips and was gone.

When I woke the next morning, actually only three hours since Joel's visit, I found that Morty had left a clipping from The New York Times on the dining room table. It was Joel Goldsmith's obituary. He died June 17, 1964, in his London hotel room. The Infinite had brought Joel home. How thoughtful of Joel to make a brief visit in New York to say farewell.

## Chapter 11

**When life's earthly chapter closes, the chapter without end begins…**

My friend Katherine Glover from Washington, D.C. wrote to me shortly after Joel passed on. She was traveling with Joel, accompanied by several teachers and students coming from London and other parts of England, the USA, the Continent, Australia and South Africa. She shared in her letter with me,

> "On Tuesday the day before Joel passed, I said to a student, don't you feel that Joel is preparing to leave us?'
>
> "Yes, I do" she answered. There was no evidence to prompt the question or indicate that the "leaving" was imminent, although for the past year Joel had given many evidences that he was preparing us for the closing of the chapter.

Katherine shared in her letter to me that in London, Wednesday morning at nine, she had a telephone call saying that Joel had passed on. Even as the telephone rang in her hotel room, with that British shrill, she had a premonition of the news.

She wrote:

> The shock was indescribable, coming just after the transcendental talks he had given, in what appeared full vitality and vigor. On the day before, he had experienced a sense of fatigue and cancelled a dinner

> engagement he and Emma planned. In the night he had some discomfort, a brief preliminary, finally, a peaceful passing in sleep.
>
> There was no *death*, only a transition, for immediately there was communication with Emma, a joyous expression of release, of freedom. Within a very short time, after the first shock and grief, all who were there felt his presence. Each of us experienced a sense of uplift, of actual joy, difficult to describe.

Some sentences later Katherine goes on,

> Immediately each one questioned: 'What can I do?' The answer was, 'Carry on.' the message conveyed was that the work would go on in every direction, with increased momentum. The most important thing each of us can do is to express, to teach what we have received.

It seemed quite natural to the group traveling with Joel, and to me, although on the other side of the Atlantic, that Joel would send such a special private farewell. After all, he was our teacher and friend. Many who were there as he passed had been in Joel's closest circle, some for 20 years or more. I had studied and meditated on Joel's works and known him personally now for more than 12 years. Joel along with some of his more advanced teachers had asked me through the years if I would be interested in becoming a teacher myself. I never felt the call to teach as a vocation. None-the-less, I had meditated for several years, by this time knowing, and asking God how I might better serve Him.

I sat in our apartment some 48 hours following Joel's passing, my spirit focusing on the challenge; "Carry on". From the moment I took Joel's message into my heart twelve years earlier I knew it was not meant for me alone. I knew intuitively that I was implored to share the Infinite Way with others. It is a message you can't outgrow, it is a message to which I was totally committed, and a message others needed.

In John 15:27 Jesus says to the disciples, "And you also are witnesses, because you have been with me from the beginning." In speaking of the disciples Jesus qualifies them as worthy of speaking on His behalf. They qualified because they had both the witness in "themselves" through the Holy Spirit, and also because they had seen the work of Jesus. I believe Joel had the very same thought in mind as he appointed us to carry his message to others.

I went to the typewriter and wrote this poem, inspired by Joel,

**If I Say So Myself**
**(I AM BLESSED)**

**I know what I am ? I know what I'm not**
**I know what I long for ? I know what I've got**
**I write lovely music ? I compose a good poem**
**I have the most wonderful husband at home**
**I'm blessed with the gift of exceptional friends**
**The caring support that their friendship extends.**
**If I make a mistake or I do something wrong**
**I can play the piano or sing a nice song**
**Or even go back to the life where I've been**
**And once again work with my fine old violin.**
**With a good sense of humor I always can know**

**When the world lets me down I'll come up with a glow.**
**If I say so myself all these things are a test**
**Of the "Infinite Way" in which I've been blessed.**

Evelyn Brill Stark

Many described Joel as a modern day St. Paul, and several devotees even suggested he was Paul's reincarnation. It would require another several chapters to share my personal thoughts. Let me say simply that Joel certainly was a St. Paul disciple. He not only held firmly in his mind Paul's own thinking, he coveted Paul's writing in his heart. Joel seemed to understand the personal anguish Paul must have experienced when he made the long trek back to Tarsus to explain to his parents why he forsook his Jewish calling to instead follow the radical teachings of a religious upstart. His parents, friends, and perhaps especially his mentor Gamaliel, all expected great things from this obviously intelligent young Jewish scholar and Rabbi. The promises and potential contribution of this Rabbi were inestimable. Surely, the thought came to Paul more than once, how will I tell them? Will they know this is of God? Will they understand that I must do things because God convinced my heart that it is right, not because of what people think? The Bible doesn't share with us the assumed ostracism that Paul most assuredly experienced.

Joel knew Paul's mind well. He, like Paul, had a Damascus Road experience. Joel met the Master and realized that he must forsake all and follow Him. In his subjugation Joel forsook the popularity and large following gained while teaching and healing in the Christian Science Church, to seek out a new direction. Joel lived the words of Jesus, which he often shared with his students, "Leave all and follow me."

Should one wonder at St. Paul's spirit abiding in Joel? I think not. God's spirit, His eternal spirit abided in Paul and being eternal abides in him still. God's spirit also abided in Joel. Therefore, I believe, it is both plausible and logical that Joel, who knew Paul intimately through his writings, could be draped with Paul's mantle. Paul and Joel were brothers, sons of the same heavenly Father. Both were reborn, given a new life, and baptized into the same Spirit. Perhaps we need reminding that there is only One Spirit and that the Spirit abided in both. Both wrote and preached the same doctrine, both pleaded with their students and disciples to "have this mind in you", that is, the spirit of God.

I recalled that Joel had mentioned in one of the lectures I attended that it would mean a great deal to him to have his message recognized by college professors. We never spoke about it, but I reflected on Katherine's words from Joel, "That now he could make the message clearer to those attuned to his consciousness." What could he possibly mean?

It became clear to me that what Joel meant was that his disciples, like those of our Lord, would at some point have received sufficient instruction and motivation to therefore aptly be capable of carrying on the ministry without Joel's physical presence.

No doubt he was convinced the professors could ostensibly radiate and in turn pass the message on to their students and in this way garner a whole new group of followers to the

Infinite Way message. I immediately sensed that this was the mission assigned to me.

When Morty came home from work that evening I shared this newly inspired project with him. I told him how strongly I felt about sharing the Infinite Way message. Without even thinking Morty promised me his full assistance saying, "I'll help you any way I can."

We discussed it for some days and then agreed that I would begin distributing audiotapes of Joel's lectures in addition to sending his books to as many influential libraries as possible. I spent countless hours researching addresses of various libraries both public and private and soon numbered almost ninety schools. I also compiled a list of tape recipients from lists of interested persons provided me by Infinite Way followers.

I became a regular visitor of a local office supplies store where I purchased address labels, packing materials, envelopes and specially designed cardboard mailing boxes to contain books or audio cassettes. Morty agreed to finance my activity and soon even became my private "mailman", making daily trips to ship books and tapes to dozens of places near and far.

That evening as I meditated I said, "Joel, I'm going to do this for you. I'm going to introduce your books to universities and seminaries, your audiotapes to a very wide audience." The next morning I purchased a college directory and thumbed through every page to note the contact person and the address of those institutions I deemed most receptive and influential.

I sent three different books over a period of six months to 88 colleges and seminaries. The books were; *The Contemplative Life, Living Between Two Worlds,* and *The Spiritual Journey of Joel S. Goldsmith.*

This is the letter I wrote to professors, librarians and seminaries.

> To the Librarian:
>
> It is with deep pleasure that I offer this book, "Living Between Two Worlds" by Joel S. Goldsmith as a gift to your library. Because Mr. Goldsmith has brought inspiration and enlightenment to so many, it is my hope that sharing it in this way, others, who feel a kinship with these ideas, may find their lives similarly enriched.
>
> I will appreciate an acknowledgment. If for any reason you cannot use this book, will you be kind enough to return it so that I can offer it to another library?
>
> Sincerely,
> Evelyn Stark

I was pleased to hear within only a few weeks that 87 of the 88 books mailed out were accepted and placed in the respective libraries. Confirmation came from as far away as the Cambridge University Library, England, Alaska, and as near as my beloved Barnard College, Columbia University in New York, where I spent four wonderful years.

In addition to sending out Joel's books and audiotapes the Spirit was leading me to begin writing again.

One Christmas, a good friend of mine, Bertha Durham, who conducted a tape group of Joel's recordings in Toronto, Canada, sent me a magazine from England, Science of Thought Review, to which she had subscribed for years and which I found very inspiring.

Bertha thought I might want to subscribe to it too. I not only subscribed to it, soon I began writing for it. Eventually over the years, 27 of my poems were published. I put them all together into a book and called it Never Apart. The Editor of Science of Thought Review at that time was Brian Graham, who printed a review of my book in the November/ December 1992 issue in Chichester, England.

**Never Apart**: Review of poems by Evelyn Stark

*Over the years, readers will be aware of the inspirational poetry of Evelyn Stark, which have appeared in the pages of the Review. Often readers have appreciatively responded to their soul-touching content. Never Apart offers us a very precious collection of 27 of Evelyn's spiritual realizations - beautifully expressed in her illumined poetic language. Herein you'll find "winged messages" which will bring Light into your darkness, a healing peace to mind and soul, and the entry of a Greater Love into the domain of your receptive heart. Here's one of my favorites:*

**Thou Art That**
**Open to the formless…**
**Invite it to carry you along the stream of blessedness to your destiny.**
**Don't struggle, don't strive.**
**Rejoice in the moment that's new and alive,**
**Nothing to think, nothing to know,**
**Love is around you wherever you go,**
**Flow with the Current, glow in the star,**
**Rest in the all of the One that you are.**

*Evelyn Stark (a faithful reader and supporter of the Review for many years) is a 12- year student of Joel Goldsmith and has put into practice the teachings of the infinite way in her everyday life. I would also like to add she is a very dear personal friend, as well as a spiritual mentor to me. I greatly value her friendship in my life and I deeply honor the beauty and richness of her soul. Never Apart makes an enriching gift from your heart to a special friend for Christmas. Do send for some copies.*

*Brian Graham.*

The result of Brian's brief tribute was most rewarding. Letters from readers of the Review came to me from all parts of the world. I had newfound friends in the Spirit from every corner of the globe. Many were students of Joel's, while others were simply writing to express our commonality and fellowship in the Spirit. I was pleased that I had addressed how I could carry the Infinite way message in this form. It convinced me again of Joel's prophetic words, "that now he could make the message clearer to those attuned to his consciousness."

Something else happened which I had never expected. My friendships established through that correspondence continue to this day. Some of the Reviews readers with whom I came in contact are persons who I've been corresponding with for more than 30 years. Most of my friends and I have never met personally, yet we enjoy a closeness nothing could alter. We are bound together as children of the Eternal.

In addition to corresponding with my spiritual family, I continue to write for the Review, which is now named New Vision, still nestled in the lovely village of Chichester. My next article will be published in the autumn of 2002 and is incorporated in the Foreword of this book.

Locally, I share Joel's message, my message, through book signing events in the Northeast, USA, and also through poetry readings at clubs and retirement villages. I was very active doing so until the autumn of 2001 when my health failed me slightly. I was unable to travel to accept the invitations extended to me. However, now in the early summer of 2002, I have again begun making short excursions to share my poetry with groups not too far distant from my retirement home here in New England.

As you would expect, my insight, long inspired and directed by Joel, has grown and taken me beyond the unfolding of my twelve years with him. I have learned more fully abide in the Spirit and to let the Spirit abide in me.

Looking back over these last four decades since Joel passed on, I humbly share John's words in his $15^{th}$ chapter that the

Spirit "Has made every provision for our fruitfulness... I appointed you to go on and bear fruit, fruit that shall last; so that the Father may give you all that you ask in my name."

I had little of the joy each child deserves when growing up, but God made a special provision for me, causing my joy to overflow as an adult, more fulfilling and enriching than one could ever think possible. I take His precious promise, to make me fruitful, to my heart asking the Father to take my written words and consecrate them in His service.

**Illumination**

**Awakening**
**Suspended in Love**
**Brushed by Angel wings**
**Nestled in Contentment**
**Free!**

Evelyn Brill Stark

# Chapter 12

## Candlewood Lake

***"Where your treasure is, there your heart will be also."***
Matthew 6:21

Let me now return to my private life with Morty these last several years. I found that I never prayed more devoutly, communicated so deeply, or confessed my love more completely as when by his side.

Morty and I were fortunate in that we had what might be called two lives together – one in New York City for close to sixty-seven years and one in Danbury, Connecticut, on Candlewood Lake for forty-two years. Candlewood Lake is the largest lake in the State of Connecticut, encompassing 5420 acres with over sixty miles of shoreline. The man made lake is 18 miles long and 2 miles wide at its widest point. The leisurely two-hour drive from Manhattan, where we lived, to Candlewood Lake, meant driving up Riverside Drive, following and crossing the meandering Hudson River, eventually following the winding country roads leading to Danbury. From late May through early September that became our weekly ritual. But it took a long ten years to find our perfect get away.

It happened this way. We had spent the first summer vacations of our married lives touring New England in a Plymouth convertible, always ending up at a resort with cottages and a hotel on a lake. We enjoyed exploring New England this way but sensed after several years that we ought to look for a lakefront cottage of our own and make it a permanent part of our lives.

No sooner said than done! We began spending every weekend searching for our dream cottage. One day we found ourselves in Danbury, Ct. and a local realtor drove us to a development called Shady Knolls. It was a small development with only seven cottages. We liked that. The cottage he showed us was not for us but we sighted our dream house from afar. Unfortunately that house was owned and occupied by three ladies who had no intention of selling. Our cottage hunting continued for ten years, but in those years we never found a house like the one we saw from afar.

Finally we stopped looking and just at the point when we gave up Morty said, "I've had enough. Let's go to Coney Island this weekend". That day a friend called and gave us the name of a very special friend, a real estate agent in Danbury, "who you should definitely contact." This made me say to Morty, "let's try one more time, as a favor to our friend." Morty agreed reluctantly.

To our amazement the realtor drove Morty and me to the same development we had visited ten years earlier, only this time what he showed us was the dream house we had sighted from afar. We couldn't believe it! I sat on the porch, looked at the lake and said to myself, "Is God here?" He was. That was it for me. We didn't notice much inside, but outside the house we were thrilled to see it had a deck, a dock and a boathouse.

Both the cottage and its location immediately captivated both of us. The day we visited the cottage that first time was a dreary drizzly one. Yet, Morty and I both agreed as we scanned the vista that, "if it looks this good when it's raining, it must be wonderful on a sunny summer day"! I pictured in my mind the vista, a glimmering lake in the mid-morning sun with forests and glens where I could walk and meditate.

Morty and I returned to New York excited about our "find". Our search had paid off. I said to Morty at dinner, "Let's put a picture window in the living room with a view of the lake." Imagine my surprise on our next visit to see that it was already there!

Now let me explain something. Morty and I were city folk. We had always lived in apartments or hotels in the city. This was a major step about which we knew nothing. Morty was apprehensive. Like most men, I suppose, he saw himself as becoming the weekend maintenance man, carpenter, plumber, and painter. In reality though, Morty's construction skills had been limited to changing the occasional burned out light bulb or taking down the living room drapes before sending them to the cleaners. In my ignorance, I never gave the eventual demands a second thought.

Because Morty was so hesitant about making such a major move, I took it upon myself to take the initiative. I called the realtor the next day and told him, "Don't show that house to anyone else. We're buying it. You get the owners to come down $1,000 and I'll get my husband to raise his offer by $1,000." And it worked! The house was ours!

Morty and I were really very fortunate. The house was sturdily constructed. Interestingly the material used for the construction all came from leftover lumber from the Barnum and Bailey Circus. We never learned the history behind the used circus lumber however; we learned that the couple that built the cottage had done so with unusual care and forethought. And the three sisters who preceded our ownership were equally committed to maintaining its sturdy charm. The sisters' life style speaks of their character. It was said that each evening they would dress formally for dinner. Fresh flowers from their garden were placed throughout the house, inside and out. That lovely scene inspired me to write;

**Lovely Flower Standing There**

**Lovely flower standing there in innocence and purity**
**What makes you so serenely still**
**So centered in your essence?**
**Can nothing touch your quiet peace?**
**Your presence seems so self complete.**
**We are so different, you and I, you're not like me at all!**
**You have no conflicts, no despair**
**But there's so much I'd like to share**
**If you could understand.**

**I touch your velvet softness and smell your fragrant breath**
**My face against you, flower,**
**We share a soft caress**
**And somehow I am blessed.**

There was a large walkout basement with a ping-pong room and windows. We had never bought a house before and consequently never gave a thought to have it inspected. We were fortunate there were no termites or mice. We felt blessed to have found a cottage where so much love and care had been bestowed.

Two weeks after signing the purchase contract we began moving our private belongings, one carload at a time from Manhattan to the cottage. Week by week the transformation took place. Family photos and coveted knickknacks were hung on bedroom and kitchen walls. Favorite bedspreads, slippers and housecoats took their place in the bedroom. The cottage was ours and our imprint was evident in every corner!

The same held true outside. When the realtor had originally asked us why we wanted the cottage we replied, "as a retreat". Morty needed it as an antidote to his hectic corporate life in the city.

One of Morty's hobbies was gracious dining. Fortunately the cottage was located in an area with many fine restaurants. Every day we'd go out for a nice lunch and it broke up the day for us. It was a serendipitous life.

Morty also loved to garden. He would plant bulbs in the autumn before the frost. In the spring daffodils and lilies bloomed first, and a few weeks later tulips ran the length of our property from the roadway to the lake. He also loved to prune the trees. Our neighbors often remarked that Morty had a natural green thumb; every tree, every branch, every twig was pruned as though in accordance with instructions from the Creator. He loved to putter around on the grounds. It was therapy for him – a respite for both of us. It meant so much to Morty that he arranged his work schedule so that for four months out of the year we were able to be at Candlewood Lake for long weekends, leaving New York Thursday afternoon, returning Monday evening.

Being alone with Morty overlooking that lake was fulfillment in itself. I was completely happy. For me it became my Walden Pond, a place so peaceful and serene that it was as close to heaven as I could come. I flourished in this life at Candlewood Lake. The beauty and peace of the surroundings enabled me to pursue my music and spiritual studies. I had the freedom and privacy to develop my inner longings most often from a chair with a view of the lake while seated on our porch. I wrote this poem seated in that chair while watching Morty putter in the garden below.

**All I Ask for in Life Is a Comfortable Chair**

**All I ask for in life is a comfortable chair**
**Indoors or outdoors – I really don't care**
**I don't want to travel or go anywhere**
**I just want to sit in a comfortable chair.**

**I've done everything and I've been everywhere**
**I've reached for the heights and I've drowned in despair**
**What I do from now on is my own affair**
**And I choose to collapse in a comfortable chair.**

In the springtime I would stroll in the early morning as the rays of the sun pushed the sleepy darkness down the shoreline and across the lake. Birds sang their wake-up songs but time stood still. Everywhere I looked buds seemed ready to spring and bloom. Leaves and ferns shimmered as the wind shook them free from dew. They became nature's wind chimes. Often I would be the first to greet a deer or wild pheasant in the gossamer brush with a hearty "good morning". I would walk aimlessly, contemplatively, thanking God for leading us to this heavenly hide-away, our little corner of the world. During that first summer on the lake I became more and more at one with God.

**To a Wood Thrush**

**Your liquid tones of melody**
**Strike deep within my soul**
**Awakening a tenderness**
**Too sweet for heart to hold.**
**My spirit reaches out to thee**
**And blends with immortality.**

Evelyn Brill Stark

There come times in each life when one senses the mystical touch of the Divine. The touch comes to us in different ways. It may come through the words of a loved one or someone we revere. Others hear God speak through His divine word or through those who interpret His love for us through the arts. It may be through inspired music, a canvas touched by a master, or through the words of a poet. More important than recognizing God's reaching out is acknowledging and responding to Him. God had used all of these forces to impact on my heart. Now He added to His touch the beauty of His creation, which so blessed me at Candlewood Lake every morning and every evening.

I was inspired to write a poem about those early spring strolls at the lake.

**Alchemy**

**Evening sunset's golden hue**
**Drifts across the lake**
**Melting what was sky of blue**
**Blending colors soft and new**
**Harmonizing space.**

**Amber, rose and violet**
**Enter – softly glow**
**Pink turns into amethyst**
**Rose has vanished in the mist**
**Where did Amber go?**

**Angel artist alchemist**
**So delicate your touch**
**You opened up my Center**
**With the colors from your brush.**

The word alchemy was used in the Middle Ages and had a magical connotation; its chief aims were to change base metals into gold. How fitting then to apply the word to the seemingly miraculous power which seeks constantly to transform us into something better. Alchemy is the hope God's Spirit expectantly sprinkles on us all.

For too many persons though, the transformation appears to be an impossibility or illusion. Those are the persons who refuse to recognize and acknowledge His being. Joel shared in a lecture in the "closed class" I attended in Los Angeles, " The nature of God is such that God only comes into manifestation through recognition. 'Acknowledge Him in all thy ways. Lean not unto thy own understanding.' This is an act of consciousness. Be still. It doesn't make any difference whether you are a saint or a sinner; when you discover God you will be white as snow and the past will be wiped out".

Often it is the intellect that keeps us from seeking God more intimately. For some it is the fear of commitment and what God might demand. Others will point to an earlier time when their love and faith was abused, shattered or destroyed. The humanist argument becomes ours – philosophy serves as a pseudo religion. Martin Luther put it more crudely, "Reason is a mistress who will serve any master." We convince ourselves that our intellect can balance and offset any and all feelings or emotions of vulnerability and dependence.

It was during the time we were moving into the cottage that I listened to a radio sermon in which the question was asked, "If your thoughts of the past week were flashed on a neon sign on Broadway, would you have to leave town?" It was a very provocative question to me. I thought especially of how shame, self-doubt and fear of exposure cause us, mistakenly, to draw on our own meager resource, the ego. The fact is that we will never measure up. Both the standards by which we are measured and the resources necessary to attain spiritual freedom are found only in surrender to God, never in ourselves. Leaning on the ego or self-understanding is like trying to find an exit on a cul-de-sac. There is none. Instead one is constantly brought back to where the search for answers to a broken and contrite spirit began.

The wonderful truth is that God never finds us deficient, and it's that great truth that sets us free. God accepts us as we are. He takes the splintered spirit and makes it whole. Joel

Goldsmith said, "The light doesn't judge darkness or condemn it or blame it for being darkness, it just dissolves it.... When God forgives our sins, God dismisses our sins... without judging, criticizing, or condemning them". There is no greater promise to soothe the anguished soul. Not a single human frailty, fear or failure is left unanswered or unsettled. What we need to recognize is that in those times of our human inability to understand we cannot seek to "lean on our own understanding".

I was fortunate that through the years I had intuitively sensed God's presence in me. I wasn't fully aware of what I was feeling but through daily meditation on sacred writings and taped lectures my spiritual search was answered. I thank God that He placed in my early life an illumined friend and counselor when I most needed him, an extraordinary man, who helped me toward the Infinite way.

Oh, how I wish I could share with you those glorious mornings, those moments when God and I walked the shores of Candlewood Lake. No doubt though, you too have had those wonderful private times - you met Him as you read Bunyan or Keats while enjoying a cup of tea. Yes, God comes to each of us in His own special time and way. The Father knows all His children and how to touch each one. As a loving Father He showers on all of us the same love – the same gift of His peace – His Presence. We all have the same inheritance. We need only claim it and to do so means simply to say yes to His call to come to Him. How tragic it is then when His children don't heed His leading.

Autumn strolls were most often taken in the cool of the evening, always in that contemplative mood wherein one can't help but to "lift the eyes unto the hills from whence cometh my help"... The waves murmured their languid autumn song. The cool fresh autumn air was resinous. The carpet on which I walked was a burst of color, multihued leaves as brilliantly intricate as the most beautiful tapestry ever woven. Summer warmth had given strength to saplings wanting now to sleep through the impending winter frost. How wonderful to know that God had invited me to join with Him on those autumn afternoons. I watched as He plucked the few remaining leaves from the trees. Soon the snow would come and He would dress them for winter.

It was during our second summer on the lake that a realization came to me. As I looked out on the lake I saw below the picture window the carpet of flowers. The seeds had been sown by Morty, as were the bulbs. Morty had repaired the boathouse and repainted the lawn furniture. The dock and deck also wore a fresh coat of paint, thanks to Morty. As I looked out the window I saw Morty walking toward a young sapling, pruning tools in hand. A remarkable transformation had taken place in the last 12 months. Our imprint was evident everywhere I looked.

It was then that the words of Jesus came to me, *"Where your treasure is, there your heart will be also."* At first I didn't understand the relevance of the words, but then it became clear.

Morty and I had purchased the cottage; we owned it! But as the months passed and we made those many weekend visits, we added more and more of ourselves to the cottage and the land. I brought brushes to paint, scrub and clean. Morty shoveled, dug, and planted. And together we transformed a cottage into a lovely home. But what struck me that day was the thought that we no longer owned that cottage, it owned us!

I saw in that transformation a similarity to how God had worked in my life. I had given myself over to Him through study and meditation. I had entered the contemplative life seeking more and more of His spirit. As I did so He pruned from me those aspects of my life that He found displeasing. He added color to those areas of my life that were drab; He added love by blessing me with Morty and a host of friends. He put music in my life and made me an instrument of His love to others. As I gave myself to Him, He was mine and we were One. It was a wonderful realization. My long and winding road had taken me through regions of pain, times of lament and periods of self-doubt. As I looked back on those periods I saw clearly that every experience had been guiding me. God's unfailing love was with me in every circumstance. In my search my faith had constantly been rewarded. What a wonderful realization that was!

It inspired me to write,

**I Surrender**

**The fragmented parts of my being, I surrender.**
**Whatever has come in between, I surrender.**
**The doubts, the hopes, the fears, I surrender.**
**The loves, the hates, the tears, I surrender.**
**Mistakes I have made through the years, I surrender.**
**All these I surrender to God.**
**What's left of my personal dreams, I surrender.**
**The beliefs, the plans, the schemes, I surrender.**
**And then when my psyche is clean, I surrender.**
**To Wholeness – to Love and to God.**

And that was the secret of my spiritual fulfillment.

## Chapter 13

### Life's last phase…

**Whoever believes in the Son has eternal life**
**John 3:36**

The last phase in the life of a couple is often the saddest period in what was a joyful, committed, lifetime together. One of the partners in a long and loving marriage may become sick or disabled. The other partner, without expecting it, suddenly becomes a primary caregiver. That happened to me after more than 62 wonderful years together with Morty. I had leaned on him throughout our marriage for years, and now it was my turn to let him lean on me. No warning had come. In fact whenever we spoke of the crisis that one or the other dying would mean in our relationship it never occurred to us that Morty might be the first to do so.

In my case, I was accustomed to him being the rock in our relationship. He made most of the important decisions about our lives. After more than sixty years of being cared for by him, I was responsible for his care.

Morty, tall and strong as he was, had fallen one day in our Manhattan home without any warning. I suspect he sensed that he was beginning to lose strength, but rather than worrying me he had kept it to himself. But soon thereafter came a second and third fall. At first he was able to raise himself upright without help. Soon though, came the time when I had to help him to his feet, and not long thereafter, others had to be called to help me. Morty, still strong mentally, did his best to maintain and display a strong spirit. In fact I remember he would not use a cane or a walker. When something had to be moved, he automatically thought, "I can do that." Once, when we were having a new chair delivered, Morty, who had difficulty walking, was suddenly going out the door. When I said, "Morty, where are you going?" he replied that he intended to help the deliveryman.

He was reluctant to accept help. He was a very proud man and I loved him for that. But now his pride was working against both of us. We loved one another and that was what helped us. This was our life together for over five years. We weren't able to go out. I was not able to leave him.

My beloved Morty became weaker and weaker. It doesn't matter what made him sick. What mattered is that he became dependent on me. This was not easy for him. Nor was it for me. Morty was used to helping other people, not being helped himself. He had been a volunteer at New York hospitals for many years. Innumerable patients had been comforted by his kindness in their time of need. Now it was his turn to be comforted.

The doctors could not provide us with any time frame so we simply took the days as they came. The unsettling circumstances broke in to remind us of the reality of our eventual physical separation. Both of us accepted that dying is a natural part of the life of an individual. We spoke of it often. We were reminded of death's approach regularly as more and more friends and family members, also in their late 70s and early 80s, were being laid to rest. Our family and community of friends were dwindling in number and becoming smaller, and with it my responsibility grew. Morty's disabling illness caused us to become more and more isolated as a couple. We knew and accepted that future communal care for Morty would in all likelihood be limited to my care for him.

Morty, knowing how difficult it was for me would try to make it easier. He never complained about any pain, and he must have had some. He tried to joke about things, was friendly with everyone. There were also many silent hours. Lovers whose lives are filled with joy know the depth of wordless fellowship. He still was a rock to me and advised me when he felt well enough. I thank God that we were together for that time period in our lives, no matter how difficult it was.

During those many months of isolation our bond of love grew ever more stronger and deeper. Optimism for a recovery waned early; however, God replaced it with a different hope and assurance. It wasn't merely a "feeling" that we would be together in death as in life; it was God's unmistakable assurance speaking to us each. God had been in and with me for many years. I often spoke to Morty about it and shared details of my spiritual discernment and illumination. Morty was more reticent about sharing his faith. I recall though that after attending a Joel Goldsmith seminar in New York, on our return to our apartment I asked him what he thought about the lecture. He replied, "It was very interesting, but what those people at the seminar are seeking, I already have!"

Morty was a highly respected businessman in New York City. Steady recognition of his abilities had brought regular promotions to positions of leadership. His business skills influenced industry in the United States and Europe alike. But it was not acumen alone that brought him notice and attention. It was his dignity, integrity and concern for others. I doubt that Morty ever raised the subject of his relationship with God when speaking with business associates. On the other hand, I am certain that none of his colleagues ever doubted that he had a spiritual side. His upright, unshakable demeanor displayed it in every business setting, even those that might be dubbed as banal.

Joel Goldsmith wrote,

"Christ Jesus, in speaking of God, referred to Him often as 'The Father within me' or 'My Father', or 'My Father and your Father'.

There was a young man who loved books and he went to a certain bookstore and bought many books. When he found the books that he wanted, he did not question the price, he paid it, and he always seemed to have enough to do this. Actually, he was a workingman, and he was probably spending for books what others may have spent on tobacco or alcohol or other forms of unnecessary living.

One day the shopkeeper spoke to him about this, asking how it was that he could buy all these books, have the books he wanted, and never be concerned about the price? But this man, evidently knowing the shopkeeper by nature and knowing that he never would appreciate the true answer said, "I have a wealthy father." That satisfied the shopkeeper and no more questions were asked. But he did not have a wealthy father. What he really was referring to was the fact that he had a God, and that God seemed to supply him with all that he had need of. His heavenly Father was rich and he was spending his heavenly Father's money. So you see he hid the truth in a fairy story, in a lie, if you want to call it that. And yet, it satisfied a man who, had he said, "Oh, God supplies me with my need," would have immediately brought forth an argument, a discussion, and probably something worse.

Joel tells another story, about Aladdin's Lamp. You remember that Aladdin only had to rub the lamp and wish and every wish came true. His every desire was quickly fulfilled. Actually, behind this is the deepest Truth of spiritual living. Everyone has, within himself, an Aladdin's Lamp. It was placed there in the beginning when he was created in the image and likeness of God. It is not a lamp at all, although the nature of it is Light. It is called Light. "I am the Light of the world." And each one, as he unfolds and manifests has within himself this divine Light, which we may call the Spirit of God. Now this, too, has many names. It has been called the Christ. Paul calls it "The indwelling Spirit." But call it by whatever name you wish, each one of us has it. Each one of us has had it from the beginning. It is a divine Spark; it is the real nature of our being. In fact, in some teachings, it is called our real Selfhood or our divine Selfhood or our divine Sonship."

If I were asked, I would describe Morty as having the divine Sonship. There was about him a forbearance and gentleness, what the New Testament calls, "The sweet reasonableness of Christ". It seemed as though Morty was ever mindful of the presence of the Lord. There was a moderation in Morty's spirit that spoke clearly of the Divine's presence in his life.

During his illness Morty's spirit continued to shine. That was God at work. Justice Hugo Black once said, "Here's hope, strength and love to those who give hope, strength, and love." That's what Morty gave to me and to all with whom he came in contact. There was no mistaking that Morty was grounded in a divine belief and experience.

I wonder if you believe that your religious experience is based on human intuition, that is to say, not based on belief primarily, but feelings and emotions. At the beginning of this century William James, the famous Harvard professor, delivered his famous lectures on the varieties of religious experience. Many have argued against, and others have added to James' 1902 treatise. Many question the notion that our senses and emotions represent a valid religious experience.

We all know how fickle our emotions can be. They ebb and flow like the tides of the ocean. It is rare to find the person whose whole life is lived in green pastures and beside still waters such as spoken about in the 23rd Psalm. Most of us find that life alternates between storm and sunshine. Believers are not immune to the fluctuation precipitated by our spiritual experience. It is something we can come to expect in our pilgrimage, especially in times of personal turmoil.

Joel Goldsmith warned against being fooled by emotions saying:

There is no such thing as a spiritual feeling. Being spiritual is the normal natural state of being alive… of being in Christ. The moment we are aware of something that is something external to what we are, it is not our self. Our self is always the pure, spiritual, natural being.

Let us not be fooled by emotions. God is not emotional, and manifested individually has no element of emotions. The I that I am has no awareness of qualities and no reaction to them. The I that I am looks out upon this world without any sense of good and evil and then lets the world define itself to the I that I am with a minimum of emotions.

Sometimes we experience exalted joy during trials and temptations, while at other times our fellowship with our Lord seems strangely distant. Sometimes we sing and sometimes we groan. St. Paul uses the phrase "We groan inwardly waiting for the new order to emerge." We need to be reminded that our ups and downs are a part of our authentic spiritual experience, especially at those times when we are not satisfied with the present experience. Sometimes we praise God while at other times we are tempted to murmur against Him. These are the daily authentic spiritual experiences we move through as we journey upward and forward as pilgrims.

We are unaware that what we need is spiritual restoration. We allow our emotions, our anxiety and fear to cloud the reality of our faith. Our human "present" overshadows our experiences in the Eternal. The lesson here is to remind ourselves that we are never separated from the mystery of time. He who is the alpha and omega is ours in the "present". Those times when we are downcast are on the human plane of emotion. Our spiritual experience on the other hand is on the eternal plane. Eternity is the solution to the riddle of emotions.

A missionary serving in India asked his Sunday School class, children aged 6 and 7, "Where is God?" Half of the class immediately pointed to the heavens while the others pointed to their hearts. We who are at one with the Infinite know that all the children were correct. God is not limited to a time or place; He is everywhere in and with us always

In the times when we allow our emotions to control we dismiss the reality of our experience. God longs to restore the spirit splintered and withered by human emotions. God the Holy Spirit reaches down to the human depths to lifts us to mystical heights.

I did not know when, but it was clear that soon I would be alone. Therefore I suppose it was quite natural during this period for me to feel downcast. I would no longer have Morty's physical presence at my side. We spent every minute together during that time. We would reminisce about the wonderful life we had enjoyed together. Then in the evening I would sing to him, kiss him good night and say, "I'll see you in the morning," never knowing if that morning would be in this life or the next.

Caring for Morty at home became more and more difficult and we moved him to a convalescent home where his last weeks would be spent. I could no longer provide the physical and medical care he needed. I visited him every day. I would sit at his bedside ending each visit by singing to him, Goodnight Sweetheart, while tenderly caressing his arm.

The day came when the doctors told me it was probably his last day on earth. In our last moments together I leaned close to him and whispered, "Morty I have something to tell you. Listen carefully. You are going somewhere soon. Nothing matters except that we love each other forever and ever. If you can communicate with me from that place you are going, do it." Then I sang to him for the last time "Goodnight Sweetheart." It was our twilight song…

It may seem natural that one should care for a loved one, especially at a time when death is near. But when one anticipates that the next step for that loved one is standing before the Lord in the Kingdom of God, that expressed love has a very different power and promise. First, the love testifies and gives witness to the divine-human partnership. Secondly, it gives witness that all are called to a shared future in that kingdom. Thirdly, it also gives praise and joy to the heart and source of all love. Finally, it confirms and strengthens our intrinsic God character, what God demands in us.

When I returned home to our apartment I sank into my favorite chair. I reflected on the past few days, difficult and trying as they had been, not to mention the last five years. The obligations and responsibilities had been more than I thought I could ever have coped with. I knew that the time had come for us to say good-bye, and I felt drained physically and emotionally.

Dr. Harry Emerson Fosdick, whose sermons we listened to early in our marriage, writes in ON BEING FIT TO LIVE WITH, "The more the output, the greater the need for replenishment and intake – that is universal law nowhere more manifestly operative than in personal experience." With Morty's departure from this world but hours distant, I prayed to God asking that He shed on me the replenishment I would need in the days ahead. There would be many demands on my time, emotions, and most especially, my spiritual experience.

The next morning I called the convalescent center and learned that Morty had gone to heaven during the night. I had a wonderful vision of Morty tall and straight, healed of all illness being welcomed by the Lord and the heavenly hosts. I thanked the nursing home staff for their many kindnesses and replaced the telephone in its cradle. A peace like none I had ever experienced enveloped me. Morty was free and I was free.

After a few minutes I took my Bible from my nightstand and I opened it to two familiar Psalms. The Psaltery had always been my favorite scriptural reading. I loved the poetic form of the songs and always found them a source of consolation and strength. Every mood known to the human heart can be found there. What my heart sought that early spring morning was a reaffirmation of the goodness of God; His active presence in healing my broken heart.

I read through both Psalm 42 and 43. Repeated in both Psalms are the words, " Why are you downcast, O my soul? Why so disturbed in me?" The words were my song of distress… But David added to his songs these words, "Put your hope in God. For I will yet praise him, my Savior and my God." The word YET jumped out at me. God reminded me in that moment that in the midst of every trial He soothes our weary spirit. The prevailing theme from the first Psalm to the last is one of thanksgiving.

When debilitating health attacks come our way, when doctors use the word terminal disease, or tell us, "He only has a few hours left", the human response is to question God's love and compassion. Many persons cry out,

"Where are you God when I need you?" Others even question His existence.

There has been no greater questioner of God's peace, presence and power than Job. The Bible tells us he was immensely wealthy. He owned thousands of animals, a large estate, employed many servants, and had been blessed with a large and healthy family. Job was greatly blessed by God and the Lord called him "the finest man in all the earth."

God, on a visit from Satan, points out Job's faithfulness and praises him. Satan replies that Job should be faithful to God, "after all you pay him so well… you protect his family… his property." The Lord tells Satan that he may cause any burden or hardship he wishes on Job, to test his faithfulness. Satan salivates at the opportunity to have Job curse God.

Job's wealth is lost as his animals are driven off, his servants killed by a band of Chaldeans, and his children crushed to death as they feast. Through it all Job remains silent even as his wife tells him to curse God.

After seven days of complete silence Job finally speaks, mocking God, "Why didn't I die at birth? I am weary of living. I will speak in my sorrow and bitterness…I would have been spared this miserable existence"

In the Old Testament Job, in his distress and time of incredible trial, addresses every question possible to God. The toll taken on his faith seemed insurmountable. Was there any consolation? How does God answer?

God responds in Job 38:

Now get ready to fight, for I am going to demand some answers from you, and you must reply. Job, how much do you know about how much I care? How much do you know about my wisdom? How much do you know about the way I order the universe...Have you ever in your life commanded the morning? Where were you when I laid the foundation of the earth? Tell me, if you have understanding....Who shut in the sea with doors...Have you entered into the springs of the sea, or walked in the recesses of the deep? Have the gates of death been revealed to you, or have you seen the gates of deep darkness? How much do you know, Job? Do you know the time the mountain goats give birth? Are you a lover of nature? Do you observe the calving of the deer? Can you count the months they fulfill, or do you know the time they give birth? Will the wild ox consent to serve you? Do you give the horse his might? Do you clothe his neck with a mane? Is it by your understanding that the hawk soars, stretching his wings toward the south? Is it at your command that the eagle mounts up, and makes his nest on high? Everything under the heaven is mine

What God is saying to Job by raising all of these questions is this: "I am a God of infinite care, love and concern for my creation."

In times where our faith might wane we can do no better than apply God's question to ourselves; "I am going to demand some answers from you..."

God's answer to me was the same as those fired at Job, " If I am concerned when the goats give birth, if I am concerned that the sun rise every morning, is it not reasonable Evelyn that I am concerned for you and Morty? I am the creator of love, life and immortality."

God assured me that He would lift me to Him and see me through the difficult days ahead. God also confirmed in that timely message to me what I had known for a long time. God is the spring from which all love flows. God had brought Morty and I together, and God would keep us together forever. It was clear to me that my inner spiritual life manifested itself outwardly as my marriage to Morty. God's words came as a divine second blessing to our union.

Those seeking comfort, love and peace will find it only in He who asked Job, "Do you know how much I care?" Solace comes from a reliance on the revealed character of God. True, we don't know all we would like to know about God, but God has revealed Himself sufficiently to us to give substance to our faith. He has revealed Himself and gives us the assurance that He is in control. Everything under the sun and above is His!

From the day Morty left, I realized he had never left. He was now living inside of me instead of outside. He was the same source of strength, joy and love I had always had. I was now free to start a new life of service, free to tell the world that there is no loss of loved ones; there is no separation except from the physical presence. And that is only temporary because LOVE ensures that Morty and I will be together again one day forever and ever.

The old gospel song speaks of my experience:

**When the darkness veils his lovely face,**
**I rest on his unchanging grace;**
**When all around me souls give way,**
**He then is all my hope and stay**

# Chapter 14

## No Separation

On March 24, 2000 – two days after my husband Morty's funeral in our home in Chester, Ct., with Morty's picture there as a reminder of his presence at the breakfast table, I wrote this poem.

**Breakfast with Morty**

**I'm eating with you Morty**
**You're eating with your wife**
**Your picture is so beautiful**
**So filled with love and life**
**That I can't doubt that you are here**
**So close – so sweet- so near – so dear**
**It really couldn't be more clear!**

**Whatever form you choose to take**
**To be with me for love's sweet sake**
**I like to think that we can touch**
**I want to feel you – oh so much!**
**To kiss your eyes, your neck, your skin**
**To make believe, is that a sin?**
**'Cause if it is – that's just too bad-**
**It keeps my heart from feeling sad**

**And snuggled in your nice warm robe**
**I feel your arms around me**
**While memories of happy things**
**We said and did surround me**
**We are so blessed to have each other**

**My sweetheart, husband, father, mother**
**There'll never ever be another**

**I love you young**
**I love you old**
**The ways I love**
**Cannot be told (can ne'er be told)**
**You are the only one for me**
**And that's how it will always be**
**For that's the truth of you and me.**

**Dedicated to our 67th Anniversary**
April 27, 2000

The fulfillment that came to me inwardly once I realized my belonging to – my oneness with God – manifested itself outwardly as my marriage to Morton Stark, the fulfillment of my life on earth. We lived and loved for almost 67 years and our union was blessed.

One morning I awoke, looked at him sleeping beside me, and God revealed Himself to me as this husband I had chosen. I said aloud, "Oh, God – you're Morty! And then, "You're EVERYONE." On reflection these many years later, I now know that it wasn't I who chose Morty; it was God who brought him to me.

In Solomon's Book of Wisdom we are instructed time and again that all righteous souls are in the hand of God.

The Book of Wisdom 3:1

> But the souls of the righteous are in the hand of God, and there shall no torment touch them.

> In the sight of the unwise they seemed to die: and their departure is taken for misery, And their going from us to be utter destruction: but they are in peace.
> For though they be punished in the sight of men,
> yet is their hope full of immortality. And having been a little chastised, they shall be greatly rewarded: for God proved them, and found them worthy for himself.
>
> As gold in the furnace hath he tried them, and received them as a burnt offering. And in the time of their visitation they shall shine, and run to and fro like sparks among the stubble.

Surely Solomon's wisdom includes those not yet with God in eternity, yet those who sense a belonging to the Eternal. Those of us living in this world, His righteous children also belong to and bask in His eternal presence now. And, if we, like those who have joined God in eternity are a part of the Eternal Presence, then we too can share in that experience wherein communication with God and other righteous souls must be seen as the highest possible blessing.

Joel Goldsmith said,

> "God is the mind of me, the Life, the Soul, the Spirit, and God is my capacity. I have access to infinite Intelligence, to infinite, eternal Life. I have access to infinite supply, infinite harmony, peace, and perfection- to all of these because I have access to infinity.
>
> A basic principle of The Infinite Way is found in the word *IS*. God Is; harmony Is; life Is; love Is; peace Is; joy Is; power Is; dominion Is because God Is. God Is

> infinite, omnipresent, omnipotent and omniscient. God already Is."

The scriptures tell us that we are born in His image; that is, we are born spiritually like Him. That likeness is Love, the love He instills in us. In that divine Love God designs our life, every facet of it, and therefore He is in every decision we make. In the design for my life He blessed me with Morty. "Did not he who made me in the womb make you (them)? Did not the same one form us both within our mothers?" Job 31:15 I dated many men, and some were serious suitors. But God had chosen for me and His plan was revealed when I met Morty. I met him on a blind date arranged by my mother and her best friend. It was love "at first sight" – (not "blind" at all!) for both of us, and a year later we were married.

I realized that if God is Morty, our life and love must be eternal. Two days after his funeral, March 22, 2000, I felt his presence and wrote the poem, "Breakfast with Morty". Since then I have felt him with me continually, loving and guiding me just as he did when he was physically present, only now he was doing it spiritually. His presence gives me a peace and joy that is beyond anything I have ever known before.

There is no incompatibility with Morty's spirit being in both heaven and with me on earth. Man invented the terms time and space. God's Loving Sprit, which is in Morty is not confined by our finite vocabulary and understanding. The purpose and power of the Spirit is not limited to, or by our inability to comprehend. Rather, God in His gracious Love to us binds our spirit to His, now and forever.

My knowledge that Morty hadn't left me actually started at the funeral when friends were invited to come to the podium and say a few words about what he meant in their lives. To my amazement one friend read a poem he claimed had come to him from Morty the night before. He read it aloud and here it is:

**"Morty I love you."**
**"I know, now let me sleep.**
**I'm right here beside you,**
**There's no need to weep.**
**I've accomplished all I wanted,**
**While you have more to do.**
**Awake we're together**
**And in sleep we are too".**

Just a few weeks later, in April, another poem wrote itself through the same human vessel.

**What would have been, is still**
**Though we're in different places**
**United as in one,**
**Crossing different spaces.**
**The April day we celebrated**
**Never need be recreated**
**Just kept inside our memory box**
**As love remembered, secured and locked.**

April $27^{th}$ was the day we were married and I feel certain that this poem came to me as an anniversary gift since it was sent to me at that time.

From then on I received poems when something special was happening in my life. I received this one the day following skin surgery,

**Like soldiers fighting in a war,**
**The army, navy, flying corps,**
**I'm proud,**
**So proud.**
**You didn't crumble like rain-drenched soil**
**Or a delicate flower tossed in boiling oil.**
**I'm proud,**
**So proud.**
**Whether things went smooth**
**Or somewhat wrong,**
**You braced yourself**
**Stayed calm and strong.**
**God has helped to pull you through**
**And eased my mind. I'm proud of you.**

And on my birthday,

**Nobody loves you like I do,**
**A bond this strong, there are so few.**
**Let's celebrate this day you came**
**Unto this earth where you remain.**
**Great powers lie within your pen,**
**The ink brings strength; renews lives again.**

And on what would have been our $68^{th}$ anniversary,

**Darling, can you feel me near**
**Hear my love song in your ear?**
**Though unseen by mortal eye**
**I'm with you – our love can't die.**

**Speaking through another's pen**
**What I feel can live again.**
**Hearken to the words of peace,**
**Bringing comfort and release.**

**Joy eternal we'll attain**
**Not a doubt should now remain.**
**On OUR day I send my heart**
**Know for sure we'll never part.**

I recently read a wonderful book by Inga L. Chesney, *Love Song from Beyond*. The book shares how Inga communicates with her beloved departed husband. In the midst of her grief comes an assurance of her husband's presence from beyond the grave. I read the book some months after Morty's passing and was intrigued by the similarity of Mrs. Chesney's experience with my own. Her husband, subsequent to his passing, gave her an anniversary present through the prompting of a friend. Mine did too! Inga's conviction that her husband was communicating with her was assured and confirmed in that he often "spoke" to her through family friends. Mine did too! And Inga writes in her book, "Thank you, God. The gifts You give are spectacular."

God's "spectacular" gift of Love demands a response, a response to Him in Who we abide, and a response to those with whom we abide. Therefore, a response and contact with those on the "other side" was not a phenomenon that seemed either foreign or strange to me. God created me in His likeness, and that likeness is, of course, in spirit. He created each of us in the same form. Consequently, both Morty and I were formed from birth in His Spirit. It would be difficult to understand and believe that our spirits, inseparable for 67 years, should all of a sudden be distant from each other.

When Morty was alive, we were on occasion forced to be separated, sometimes for days or even weeks. But yet when we were joined again, we were often amazed when sharing with each other the activities of each during our separation, that there were so very many activities that needed not be mentioned. Each of us was already intuitively aware of so much that had taken place, without speaking about it.

When I think of a person passing to the "other side" my mind goes immediately to Manhattan when my sister and I sailed to Europe as teenagers. I recall we left Pier 59 aboard the French Line's De Grasse, with the next stop being Le Havre, France. There was great excitement both aboard the ship and below, on the dock. Champagne bottles were uncorked, an orchestra was playing and colorful streamers and confetti bedecked the giant ship's bow. Tugboats towed us into the Hudson River where smaller boats saluted the proud lady on which we were sailing with air horns and whistles.

Our ship slid ever so slowly from its slip and the stern was towed upriver. When the turn was completed the ship sent out three great blasts into the air! They were, at least in my mind, first, a farewell to New York, then, a warning to all those many smaller boats to make way, and for the passengers? It was the signal to us that we were off and the next stop was the "other side", Europe.

The ship lumbered southward, suddenly no longer tethered, free of the many ropes that held it taut and encumbered to the several tugboats. At first it seemed as though the ship was reluctant to engage its enormous engines and great force to break free from land. I remember thinking that it was as though the ship was obeying the hearts of the many passengers and their loved ones on the dock. No separation! But, then it began to move, slowly at first, finally under its own steam, as though it was bound to both a schedule and destination. It began to move steadily and more speedily sending an ever-larger wake breaking from its bow, past lower Manhattan, the Statue of Liberty, Staten Island and then into the wide-open Atlantic.

We stood on the deck waving to those on the dock, and to strangers passing in pleasure craft, and to sightseers aboard the Circle Line, excited to finally be under way. Yet, we both sensed the angst that accompanied an Atlantic crossing in those early years of international travel. For most onboard there was, I believe, the thrill and excitement of traveling to "parts unknown", but paradoxically, the fear of being bound for distant and unfamiliar shores. We were leaving the comfort and security of what was known, for strangers, cultures, and parts unknown.

Reflecting on it now, it strikes me as being very similar to leaving and saying a final farewell to a loved one. There is naturally the sadness in having to say good-bye to the physical presence, not knowing when the final reconciliation will come. But there is also the feared loneliness that suddenly becomes a reality. Habit bids to set a place at the table, suddenly a place no longer needed. The seven decades long love ritual of turning at the front door to share a smile and blow a good-bye kiss, now meets an empty room. The table where family tradition and holidays were celebrated would now have one too many chairs.

Darkness came as we sailed with Long Island becoming a distant shore, variegated lights stretching along on our left. Miles behind was Manhattan, our home. The ship's dinner bell clanged but I decided to make one more visit to the deck for a final look, knowing that the only view for the next ten days would be the open sea. I told my sister I would join her for dinner in a few minutes.

I could no longer see New York City and the flickering lights along the south shore of Long Island were now few and far apart. I recall though that there was a glow, a sort of halo suspended in the far distant west. A deckhand passed as I stood at the ship's rail and I asked him what the lights were. He replied in a French accent, "What you see there, beyond the horizon, Madame, are the lights of Manhattan reflected in the clouds, in the skies." I thought to myself, God has given me a sign, a kind of symbol, His reflection, to remind me that it's all still there. Nothing has changed.

In the first letter I received from home once in Europe I learned that my mother, Selma, and family friends had remained at the dock until the ship was almost out of sight. They then left the dock and traveled to lower Manhattan and watched the SS De Grasse from Battery Park until we were out of sight beyond the horizon. They told of how the ship, the largest sailing out of port that afternoon was "so majestic looking". Then as it steamed along the Hudson and into the open sea the ship appeared smaller and smaller; "all we could see on the horizon were the smokestacks, then only the belching smoke, and then finally only a speck."

In reality nothing of course had changed. The grandness and size of that huge ship had not changed. The two enormous smokestacks, the huge anchors weighing many tons, the immense bulk that comprised the ship's living areas had not changed. It was the perception that had changed.

In a similar way that is what occurs when we must say good-bye. Yes, the physical presence is no longer there, but yet, the spirit both remains with us and also moves to the Godhead. It is a matter of perception, grounded in faith, and a part of God's grand plan.

In the book *Introduction of Spiritism*, Allan Kardek translates the work of Anna Blackwell and writes; "Each of us is temporarily provided a perishable envelope wherein our spirit will reside, the destruction of which, by death, restores them to liberty. God has chosen the human species for the incarnation of spirits arrived at a certain degree of development; it is this which gives it a moral and intellectual superiority to all the others. The soul is an incarnated spirit, whose body is only its envelope."

Freedom of the spirit is the release of the soul to move into experiences beyond both human restrictions and comprehension. St. Paul reminded us that in our human experience God restricts our vision of the beyond; we see at best "darkly". And Joel reminds us of our limitations to "see" and wrote in a letter to Lorraine Sinkler in August, 1963, "I witness that the "natural man" is a prisoner of the mind, locked in his own man-made rules and regulation's misnamed laws – and Grace sets him free." The journey into "Freedom" is sought outside our natural self, within, in the soul. That is where God's Spirit and our spirit are free to act, to live as One. There the soul is freed from what our natural self is, and therefore free to meet and commune with other freed souls.

Joel Goldsmith spoke of this to a small group of students in Hawaii on September 30, 1963, just a few days before leaving for London, England,

> "…You have brought yourself to my consciousness. Therefore, I have been in your consciousness and you have been in my consciousness, and what we have experienced of each other is this consciousness, this spiritual companionship… because in the kingdom of God there is a union… This (spiritual) relationship is an eternal relationship." The assurance of that eternal

relationship is promised to us by Jesus in Matthew 28:20, "And surely I am with you always (My Spirit) to the very end of the age."

Inga Chesney wrote in *Love Song from Beyond*, "Every day there is a light shining somewhere; we just have to look for it, let it enter our heart, and keep it warmly lit with all the things that are good."

What could be more "good" than knowing that love and lovers will never part? What could be more special than to commune with that loved one with whom a lifetime has been shared? What could be more wonderful than being wed to the Eternal?

**NO SEPARATION**

**If Love and Death walk side by side**
**I'll take them both within my stride**
**Because I know the truth, you see,**
**That nought can take what's mine from me**
**And Love exists eternally.**

**If Love and Death can tear apart**
**And crush and kill the breaking heart**
**I will not long the victim be nor will I let this misery**
**Conceal the truth I know to be**
**Our Love is for eternity.**

Evelyn Brill Stark

## Chapter 15

### Have this Mind in You

One of Joel's oft repeated phrases was, "Have this mind in you, which was also in Christ Jesus." (St.Paul)

Joel's personal commitment to Jesus Christ, as Lord and teacher, could not be missed. He lived according to what had been revealed through scripture and the leading of the Holy Spirit. He truly sought to have Christ's mind and to live accordingly. Joel's life had a profound influence on me, as on all of his students.

Joel, like me was born Jewish and had come to faith in Jesus Christ in mid-life. Like St. Paul, he turned his attention, affection and attitude toward Jesus as mature adult in his mid-30s. Joel's teaching was that of St. Paul saying that one must give over control of one's mind to the leading of the Infinite.

Following my visit to California, I wrote Joel sharing that the "closed" class had caused me to reanalyze my commitment to the Infinite, seeking to "Have the mind of Christ." I explained that the concept was new to me. During the years prior to studying and following the Infinite Way message I had read a great deal about the Christian way, and often attended Christian church services. The reading and messages, for the most part, spoke of leading a moral and upright life, with Jesus as our example. However, few ever referred to this life style as holy, or suggested one had to have a new "mind".

I asked Joel to send me material and recommendations on how I could seek this change in my life. My sense was that my motivation was pure but unfocussed. He immediately sent me a suggested reading list along with several of his articles. He had devotees teaching in all major North American cities and suggested those on the East Coast with whom I might study. I was flattered to think that Joel would take such personal interest in me. He even hinted that perhaps I might want to study further in preparation to becoming a teacher of The Infinite Way.

In one of Joel's Newsletters he wrote:

> "Make the contact and you will find God's Grace flowing and never will you have to tell God what you need or want…
>
> Paul revealed much of this to me when he made it so clear that you're not children of God, except "if so be the Spirit of God dwell in you"… when that same human being receives the Spirit of God in him, then does he become the Son of God, then does he live under God's Grace.
>
> Therefore, it behooves us not to go round prating about God, talking about God, but attaining God realization, living and moving and having our being in the Word until the Spirit, Itself, takes over and begins to live our life. There, too, it was Paul who told us, "*I* live, yet not I. Christ liveth my life."

God must be to us a living experience. And the Bible must be to us a living book.

The man of earth becomes that man who has his being in Christ. The unillumined becomes the illumined. The man living in darkness becomes the Light of the world. The man living in sin, disease, death, poverty, becomes the Son of God, and thereby, an heir of God, joint heir to all of heaven!"

I studied and meditated on all that Joel sent me. I did so to become more "perfect" while preparing for the next visit with Joel just a few months hence. I sought a contrite spirit. I listened to his audiotapes daily while also reading *The Infinite Way*. I had to unlearn what my natural mind held and be transformed to a new level where my thoughts were no longer mine alone. An unfolding occurred as I sought a "new" mind; I began to assume a new spiritual nature. My old nature was being replaced – my resistance crumbling.

God tells us through St. Paul in the New Testament,

"… consider yourselves dead to sin (your human living) and alive to God in Christ Jesus."

This means giving over one's control to God, and this begins with giving over the mind, one's will. It is letting the human will wane and God's will become the soul's desire.

**Relationships**

**You play my music**
**You write my poem.**
**You smile your disguise in my husband's eyes**
**Caressing and blessing my home.**
**You want me to be happy**
**And beautiful and true.**
**Your gifts you give so I can live**
**The way you want me to.**

**What would you have me to do?**
**My life belongs to you.**

Evelyn Brill Stark

Having Christ's mind is to be holy. The call to be holy, of which Paul urges all believers, comes from God Himself;

Be holy because I, the Lord your God, am holy. (Leviticus 19:2 as quoted in 1st Peter 1:16)

The supreme attribute of God is His holiness and this is the state of grace to which He seeks to lead us. It is called sanctification or holiness. The word sanctify has its roots in the Latin words, sanctus, holy and facere. The Old Testament's words are grounded in a verb one can translate as, "separation from other things". This means something or someone placed into a realm or category separated from what is common or profane; set apart from the ordinary.

St. Paul tells us in Romans 12:2 that we are to,

"be transformed by the renewal of your mind."

Paul was not referring to a change in the human mind, the seat of logic and reason. Rather, he refers to the transformation of the will, wherein we receive God's gift of the spiritual "mind", that which guides our thinking and actions.

In Romans 6:4, Paul writes,

> "We were…buried with him… into death in order that, just as Christ was raised from the dead through the glory of the Father, we too may live a new life…"

Of being perfect the New Testament (Paul) says,

> "He who is born of God and God's Spirit (seed) abides in Him." 1 John 3:9

They are now perfect or complete. They are perfect because God has perfected them, made them new.

In Second Corinthians 5:17 Paul writes,

> "Therefore, if anyone is in Christ he is a new creation, the old has passed away, behold the new has come."

It is difficult to imagine oneself as a saint in this life, yet in the scriptures God calls us to be "perfect". Paul speaks of God's challenge, to our being perfect, when he writes in Philippians speaking to recent converts:

> "Have this mind in you which was also in Christ Jesus…If you have any encouragement from being

> united with Christ, if any comfort from His love, if any fellowship with the Spirit, if any tenderness and compassion, then make my joy complete by being *like-minded*, having the same love, being one in spirit and purpose."

Paul was speaking to a group but his instructions were for each individual. You may be familiar with the adage, "you become what you think about most of the time". For me this meant that I was to realign my allegiance, reallocate my time, and redirect my resources.

I learned that to be filled with the Spirit I needed to withdraw from time to time in order to replenish that which was being expended. I also had to learn to pray. Prayer did not come naturally. To assume one knows how to pray might well be the height of folly. Even the disciples, those who walked daily with the Lord asked Him to teach them how to pray. Luke 11:1

Prayer, in its purest form, became easier as I practiced it. I sought to enter God's sanctuary through different methods and finally settled on a threefold approach. First I would simply bask in His glory, the awesomeness of the Creator. Then I would exclaim my joy in being one with Him. Finally I would make my plea for help known, which was actually the most instinctive tendency, which I'm sure He knew. My reason for voicing my needs last was simply to first honor God, for Who He was in my life. Each prayer ended with a plea that the Infinite help me become a new creature, a new person in Christ.

I understood that I was a new person transformed from what I had been. It seemed fitting that Joel used this verse so often because I, and no doubt others, needed constant reminding of how we might best honor God. Honoring God required submission to His will and that could only come about by seeking to be like Jesus, by seeking to become perfect.

The word "perfect" used in Matthew 5:48 and Philippians 3:15 means, "spiritually mature." Spiritually mature followers overcome sin and temptations by continually doing good. It is what is conveyed in the Old Testament telling us of how our inner life ought to be constructed,

"… as he thinketh within himself, so is he…" Proverbs 23:7

The prerequisite for a holy life begins in the mind, a well-ordered disciplined mind. I recall hearing Joel say, "Christ is the activity of Truth in consciousness."

The Greek word used in the Bible to describe this change is "metanois", that is, a transformation of the mind. It is the "move" from our logical reasoning mind to the spiritual mind. (God's mind in us). That gift can only be received by denying our own will by seeking God's mind, no longer remaining on the human logical plane. It demands, says Russell Henry Stafford in his, *We Would See Jesus*,

> "self-discipline for the encouragement of thoughts aimed at pure ideals and to the exclusion of thoughts arising from that rebellious instrument of the human will…" (our human mind)

I learned that the realization of sainthood, a spirit perfectly attuned to the Infinite, is both demanded and achievable in the present life. God would never beckon a soul to something unattainable. To be clear though, it is not attainable in our own strength. God's Holy Spirit serves as guide, teacher and the source of strength in moving us to become perfect.

I began reading about both contemporary Christians and about the lives of past Christians to help me shape an understanding of Gods will. I read from Merton, Barclay, and Wesley. My main authority, however, was the Bible. I found in God's words both the precepts and the promise.

For some, the salvation experience (justification and new birth) and sanctification occur at the same time, particularly in the older, mature person. I suppose this is due the fact that one has been seeking for some years and come to a conclusive understanding. Further, one has adopted certain disciplines which the mind and will have accepted. For most, however, sanctification is subsequent to justification and comes about slowly over a period of time, a time of earnest seeking.

John Wesley calls sanctification a "state of grace." He implies that there is no fixed point or degree of conclusion. Holiness is a constant seeking, a gradual progression which extends beyond this life into eternity.

For me, it took many months to come into a "state of grace", wherein it became my consciousness. It continues to unfold to this day. Holiness cannot be rushed. It is a constant seeking, its perfection not completed until one stands in the presence of the Eternal. In the same way that we are justified by faith, we are sanctified by faith. In both instances the verb leads our spirit to fulfillment wherein both salvation and sanctification become a state (noun) of being.

In Colossians 3:1 Paul repeats what is expected of us,

> "Since, then, you have been raised with Christ, set your hearts on things above, where Christ is seated at the right hand of God."

These Biblical statements remind us that we have died with Christ, died to our former selves, and are reborn in His image, having and abiding in His Spirit.

Sanctification is the process by which one grows fuller and richer in union with Christ. It is the step by which, "we will in all things grow up into him who is the Head, that is Christ… Eph 4: 15. Paul sums this up again in Corinthians 1:30

> " It is because of him (God) that you are in Christ Jesus, who has become for us wisdom from God – that is, our righteousness…"

Be ye holy…

# Chapter 16

## A Messianic Jew

**"Whoever acknowledges me before men, I will also acknowledge him before my Father in heaven.**
Matthew 10:32

Many readers of this book will be interested in how I, born into a Jewish home, came to a belief in Jesus Christ as the Messiah. Most readers probably acknowledge the historical Jesus, but perhaps not as the Messiah, King of the Jews. I want to share in this final chapter that I believe in both the historical and the resurrected Jesus. I am somewhat reluctant however, to share how this spiritual insight and experience came about for two reasons. Yet, I am compelled to do so because as stated in the bold heading above, I must "acknowledge *Him* before *you*."

First, my reluctance to share too much stems from my wish not to venture too far from the purpose of this book, that is, to highlight my search for the Infinite through my studies with Joel Goldsmith. However, Joel, who was also Jewish and who believed Jesus Christ was the Messiah, spoke openly and warmly of his relationship with Jesus Christ and referred to Jesus' example as being the key in how to lead one's life.

Secondly, coming to an acceptance of Jesus Christ as the Messiah was a decade's-long journey for me. To explain the search in too few words may result in less than a complete understanding. None-the-less it is my hope that this short explanation will inspire both the believer and non-believer alike to seek further.

Theologians suggest that a person comes to a belief and religious conviction through; tradition, the Bible, and the leading of the Holy Spirit. I had no religious training in my home. Although my parents and my husband were Jewish we did not practice the religion, and worship was limited to occasional visits to Sunday School and Holy Day services at our Temple. I did, however, as you will have read, begin a search for the Infinite early in life. Initially it was through study and meditation, delving into various traditions. In time I found that only the Judeo-Christian teachings soothed my soul's longing. It was through the Bible, my study of the Old and New Testament, not tradition, that I came to a belief. A mood of acceptance was cultivated in me through my regular reading of the Gospels and other religious literature. This path, coupled with my 12 years of studying Joel Goldsmith's message, also brought me into a relationship with the Holy Spirit.

I am a Messianic Jew, one who is Jewish and believes that Jesus Christ was the Messiah foretold in the Old Testament. I believe Jesus Christ was a historical person, a Jew, God's chosen servant, and whose messianic role Old Testament writers heralded.

*The Historical Jesus*

Most convincing to me was to learn that the coming of the Messiah was announced in, and permeates many portions of the Old Testament. It is replete with messianic themes. The Messiah's history, His coming, along with His role are all announced by Jewish Prophets. The New Testament is the unfolding of those Old Testament promises. It is where history's prophesies come alive through Christ's living the Messiah's role.

I trust that you, the reader, agree that there can be little doubt about the historical Jesus having lived and acted for more than thirty years. In addition to the life of Jesus as recorded by the Jewish New Testament writers and the Gentile physician Luke, however, should one seek further evidence one can also turn to historical writers of the same period, the most noteworthy being Tacitus.

> On July 19-27, A.D. 64, a great fire destroyed Rome; only four of its fourteen quarters remained intact. The Roman populace blamed the Emperor Nero. There were false rumors that he had been singing songs about the burning of Troy. To get rid of these stories, Nero blamed the Christians. The Roman historian Tacitus explains what happened:
>
> But all human efforts, all the lavish gifts of the Emperor, and the propitiations of the gods, did not banish the sinister belief that the conflagration was the result of an order (Nero). Consequently, to get rid of the report, Nero fastened the guilt and inflicted the most exquisite tortures on a class hated for their abominations, called 'Chrestians' by the populace. Christus, from whom the name had its origin, suffered the extreme penalty during the reign of Tiberius at the hands of one of our procurators, Pontius Pilate… (the Christians) Covered with the skins of beasts, they were torn by dogs and perished, or were nailed to crosses, or were doomed to the flames and burnt, to serve as a nightly illumination, when daylight had expired.

Why did Nero blame the Christians? The answer may be that they were living near the place where the fire started: the eastern part of the Circus Maximus. Further, Nero could never punish the Jews of Rome: there were thousands of them. The Christians, on the other hand, were an easy target.

The great fire occurred some 30 years following the death and Resurrection of Jesus. Clearly Tacitus believed that Jesus was a historical figure.

Christians were no longer a small group of Jews who followed the teachings of Jesus, but were now found in every corner of the Roman Empire and beyond. Nowhere in the Bible is the term "Christian" used; it became assigned to those who believed that Jesus Christ was the Messiah. The title "Christians" was not applied, however, until after the death, resurrection and ascension of Jesus. The term was used in the same way as the term "Palestinians" was applied to those who lived in Palestine. It should be noted that Jesus and his Jewish followers observed, to the letter, all Jewish tradition and religious practices.

If the historicity of Jesus could have been disproved Christianity would have been buried and never resurrected. Theologians tell us that a new religion was born weekly, most in the shadow of the destroyed Temple in Jerusalem. Few of these new religions however, lived beyond Jerusalem's walls or for more than a matter of weeks. Christianity though, we know, spread to the uttermost parts of the world and continues to this day.

Not everyone though, who accepted Jesus' historical reality accepted his Messianic role, particularly many of Jewish faith and tradition.

Rabbi Leo Bæck, a leading philosopher-theologian and historian of religion, though sharply rejecting Christianity, none-the-less supports the notion of a historical Jesus and declared the Jewishness of Jesus. He emphasized that Jesus was a Jew, born among Jewish people and recognized by other Jews of his time:

> Most portrayers of the life of Jesus neglect to point out that Jesus is in every characteristic a genuinely Jewish character, that a man like him could have grown only in the soil of Judaism, only there and nowhere else. Jesus is a genuine Jewish personality, all his struggles and works, his bearing and feeling, his speech and silence, bear the stamp of a Jewish style, the mark of Jewish idealism, of the best that was and is in Judaism, but which then existed only in Judaism. He was a Jew among Jews; from no other people could a man like him have come forth, and in no other people could a man like him work; in no other people could he have found the apostles who believed in him.

Other prominent Jewish religious leaders and scholars concur, some suggesting that Jesus was indeed the long awaited Messiah.

> As a child I received instruction both in the Bible and in the Talmud. I am a Jew, but I am enthralled by the luminous figure of the Nazarene. Albert Einstein, Nobel Prize winner in physics; former professor, Princeton University

I couldn't help writing on Jesus. Since I first met Him, He has held my mind and heart.... Everything He ever said or did has value for us today, and that is something you can say of no other man, alive or dead... He became the Light of the world. Why shouldn't I, a Jew, be proud of it? Sholem Asch, Yiddish novelist and author:

It is a peculiar manifestation of our exile-psychology that we permitted, and even aided in, the deletion of New Testament Messianism, that meaningful offshoot of our spiritual history. It was in a Jewish land, that this spiritual revolution was kindled; and Jews were those who had spread it all over the land.... We must overcome the superstitious fear which we harbor about the Messianic movement of Jesus, and we must place the movement where it belongs, namely, in the spiritual history of Judaism.... Martin Buber, author and former professor at Hebrew University, Jerusalem

Neither Christian protest nor Jewish lamentation can annul the fact that Jesus was a Jew, an Hebrew of the Hebrews. Surely it is not wholly unfit that Jesus be reclaimed by those who have never unitedly nor organizedly denied him, though oft denied by his followers; that Jesus should not be so much appropriated by us as assigned to the place in Jewish life and Jewish history which is rightfully his own. Jesus was not only a Jew but he was the Jew, the Jew of Jews.... In that day when history shall be written in the light of truth, the people of Israel will be known not as Christ-killers, but as Christ-bearers;

> not as God-slayers, but as the God-bringers to the world. Rabbi Stephen S. Wise, Zionist leader and founder of the Jewish Institute of Religion (Rabbi Wise was Rabbi when I on occasion would visit a Temple in New York as a young adult)

> Perhaps, too, in this enlightened age, as his mind expands, and he takes a comprehensive view of this period of progress, the pupil of Moses may ask himself, whether all the princes of the house of David have done so much for the Jews as that prince who was crucified on Calvary. Benjamin Disraeli, Former Prime Minister of Great Britain

What a wonderful solace I found in reading what these great Jewish leaders and teachers said about my Messiah. Most persuasive though, to me, is The New Testament that confirms Jesus' Jewishness in stating that He was born in Bethlehem to a young Jewish girl named Miriam (Mary). The maternal lineage established His Jewishness.

His Place of Birth

> So Joseph also went up from the town of Nazareth in Galilee to Judea, to Bethlehem the town of David, because he belonged to the house and line of David. He went there to register with Mary, who was pledged to be married to him and was expecting a child. While they were there, the time came for the baby to be born, and she gave birth to her firstborn, a son. Luke 2:4

Jewish marital tradition suggests that Miriam was in her early teens when she gave birth. From the moment of his birth to his circumcision, his pidyon ha ben ceremony (on the eighth day), his bar mitzvah, his d'roshes in the synagogues, and even to his final epitaph, the crude sign fixed over his head on the cross, "Jesus Of Nazareth, The King Of The Jews," was identified with the Jewish people.

*The Historical Jesus and His Messianic Role*

Accepting Jesus' Jewishness as I do, I feel it helpful to highlight the Old Testament references to the Messiah's coming and the New Testament's answers.

The main theme of the Bible is the Messiah, so it shouldn't surprise us that God had already revealed the truth about the Messiah through the prophets. When God, in about 700 B.C., revealed to the prophet Micah that the Messiah would be born in the town of Bethlehem, he also disclosed that the one who would be born in the form of man existed long before in the Godhead (Father, Son, and Holy Spirit):

> But you, Bethlehem, though you are small among the clans of Judah, out of you will come for me one who will be ruler over Israel, whose origins are from of old, from ancient times.' Micah 5:2 (OT)

*The Messiah's Role*

The prophet Isaiah describes the characteristics of the Messiah with the different names to be given:

> For to us a child is born, to us a son is given, and the government will be on his shoulders. And he will be called *Wonderful Counselor, Mighty God, Everlasting Father, Prince of Peace*. Of the increase

> of his government and peace there will be no end. He will reign on *David's* throne and over his kingdom, establishing and upholding it with justice and righteousness from that time on and for ever. Isaiah 9:6-7

*The Messiah's Lineage is established*

The Messiah was born as a man and his Jewish lineage is provided to us in detail in the first chapter of the New Testament. In accordance with the prophets, he is

> the son of Abraham, the son of David and the son of Mary.

Consequently, the claim that He will "reign on David's throne… (the earthly throne) and forever (the heavenly throne at God's right hand).

*The Blessing to All People*

God promises to bless Abraham and his family in the very first part of the Old Testament. Jesus is the seed of Abraham and through Him,

> I will make you into a great nation and I will bless you; I will make your name great, and you will be a blessing. I will bless those who bless you, and whoever curses you I will curse; and all peoples on earth will be blessed through you. Genesis 12:2

The Children of Israel were the chosen community through which would come the Savior of the World, Jesus the Messiah, the Holy One sent from God to ransom mankind. The Messiah was to be born among the descendants of Abraham, Isaac, and Jacob -- the Children of Israel. They were called to be holy and unique from all other nations.

The prophetic words of Isaiah are found in his 40th chapter where it is written,

> the voice of one crying in the wilderness: prepare the way of the Lord.

In the same chapter we read,

> Behold my servant, whom I uphold, my chosen, in whom my soul delights; I have put my spirit upon him, he will bring forth justice to the nation.

The Messiah IS and always HAS BEEN

In the beginning was the Word, and the Word was with God, and the Word was God. He was with God in the beginning. Through him all things were made; without him nothing was made that has been made. In him was life... John 1:1

John says clearly that God and His Word could not be separated. The Word was God from the beginning – there being, of course, no beginning. God, the Word, has always been.

When God created the universe, the Word he spoke was one with Him. We cannot separate God from his Word. This eternal Word of God, who is one with Him and contains all His attributes, was revealed in Jesus, the son of Mary, as it is written:

> The *Word* became flesh and made his dwelling among us. We have seen his glory, the glory of the One and Only, who came from the Father, full of grace and truth. John 1:14

There was life in the Word of God, and wherever the Word became present, life was created in all its different forms.

*Word* in this instance is translated from the Greek word Logos, meaning; truth's genesis and it is the seat of all pure reason and the root of our word logic. This is why Jesus spoke of Himself being the Truth.

Even as I write these words, the same holds true for me, of course in a much less significant way. I cannot be separated from my words. My words represent me and all that I am. God, through His Word, His eternal existence, also abides in me.

*The Messiah speaks of His authority*

> I and the *Father* are one. John 10:30

There are several references to the Father by Jesus recorded in Matthew. Best known is, of course, the Lord's Prayer. Then there is the oft recited,

> For whosoever does the will of my Father in heaven… Math.12:50,

and there is the transfiguration moment when God says,

> This my Son, whom I love, with him I am well pleased…Math. 17:5

There are also the references in the 27th chapter where Jesus, at the crucifixion moment has claimed to be the Son of God, and the acknowledgement by one of the Centurions,

> Surely, he was the son of God.

"We certainly do not get in the Hebrew Bible any teacher speaking of God as 'Father'... like the Jesus of Matthew. And this habitual and concentrated use rightly produces upon us an impression ... we are moved by it to wish that we too could feel that doctrine, even as Jesus teaches that we ought to feel; and that we, too, could order our lives in its light and by its strength." C.G. Montefiore Reform Jewish scholar

The question was asked of Him,

> Are you greater than our father Abraham? (Abraham lived around 2000 BC) He died, and so did the prophets. Who do you think you are? Jesus replied, "...Your father Abraham rejoiced at the thought of seeing my day; he saw it and was glad." You are not yet fifty years old," they said to him, "and you have seen Abraham!" "I tell you the truth," Jesus answered, "before Abraham was born, I am!" John 8:56-58

Those who heard that extraordinary statement learned not only that His existence preceded the birth of Abraham, but also His declared deity. The human man Jesus declares the divine Man, Son of God.

The most striking feature of the teaching of Jesus is that he was so frequently talking about himself. Jesus set Himself apart from other great religious figures who were self-effacing while Yeshua was self-advancing. Others would direct people away from themselves and to "the truth." They couched their teachings in such phrases as, "From my understanding, that is the right thing to do." In contrast, Jesus said, "I am the truth, follow me."

If Jesus (Yeshua) was not the Messiah as he claimed, he was certainly the most arrogant and blasphemous rabbi of all history.

Yeshua didn't present the "many different sides" to the questions posed. He spoke to each issue directly and authoritatively. He did not need to present many opinions to be weighed and considered. He delineated what was true in simple forthright statements.

He believed that Old Testament prophecies about the Kingdom of God and the time and method of salvation were being fulfilled in His own ministry. He taught that the role of the Jewish nation as the people of God was transferred to those who accepted Him as the Messiah and lived His teaching.

*The Messiah's entry into Jerusalem –Preceding the Crucifixion*

The Old Testament tells us of the coming of Zion's King in Zechariah 9:9 "

> Rejoice greatly, O Daughter of Zion! Shout, Daughter of Jerusalem! See, your king comes to you, righteous and having salvation, gentle and riding on a donkey, on a colt, the foal of a donkey.

Matthew 21 (New Testament) tells us:

Jesus sent two disciples, saying to them,

> Go to the village ahead of you, and at once you will find a donkey tied there, with her colt by her. Untie them and bring them to me. If anyone says anything to you, tell him that the Lord needs them, and he will send them right away. This took place to fulfill what was spoken through the prophet: "Say to the Daughter of Zion, 'See, your king comes to you, gentle and riding on a donkey, on a colt, the foal of a donkey.' " …The crowds that went ahead of him and those that followed shouted, "Hosanna to the Son of David!" (Confirmation of the lineage)

*The Messiah's Leading to the Crucifixion*

Other Old and New Testament themes offer similarly mirrored images. The first promise of salvation is found in Genesis, the very first book of the Old Testament, written by Moses.

Genesis 3*:* 14,15

> So the Lord God said to the serpent, "Because you have done this, Cursed are you above all the livestock and all the wild animals! You will crawl on

> your belly and you will eat dust all the days of your life. And I will put enmity between you and the woman, and between your offspring and hers; he will crush your head, and you will strike his heel."

This early Biblical passage is called protevangelium, meaning "first gospel.", the first good news, God's promise that the head of the serpent would be trampled pointed forward to the coming of the Messiah and God's ultimate victory over the tempter. It is Christ who will tramp on the snake; it is He who will be forced to endure the pain on the cross, Whose heel will be stricken.

The prophet David forecasts Christ's death in Psalm 22:16

> I am poured out like water, and all my bones are out of joint. My heart has turned to wax; it has melted away within me. My strength is dried up like a potsherd, and my tongue sticks to the roof of my mouth; you lay me in the dust of death. Dogs have surrounded me; a band of evil men has encircled me, they have pierced my hands and my feet. I can count all my bones; people stare and gloat over me. They divide my garments among them and cast lots for my clothing.

The New Testament parallel,

> When they had crucified him, they divided up his clothes by casting lots. Matthew 27:35

David wrote his words even though crucifixion was not yet used as a method of execution in his day. It was invented much later and was used by the Romans during the time of the Messiah.

The Messiah himself confirmed on a number of occasions that he came to give his life as a ransom *(fida)*. He said about himself:

> For even the Son of Man did not come to be served, but to serve, and to give his life as ransom for many. Mark 10:45

John the Baptist *(Yahya Ibn Zakaria),* Jesus' cousin, lived at the same time as the Messiah. He was sent by God to prepare the way for the Messiah as foretold by Isaiah:

> A voice of one calling:
> In the desert prepare the way for the LORD; make straight in the wilderness a highway for our God. Every valley shall be raised up, every mountain and hill made low; the rough ground shall become level, the rugged places a plain. And the glory of the LORD will be revealed, and all mankind together will see it. Isaiah 40:9-11
>
> You who bring good tidings to Jerusalem, lift up your voice with a shout, lift it up, do not be afraid; say to the towns of Judah, "Here is your God!" See, the Sovereign LORD comes with power, and his arm rules for him. See, his reward is with him, and his recompense accompanies him. He tends his flock like a *shepherd:* He gathers the *lambs* in his arms and carries them close to his heart; he gently leads those that have young.

The Messiah did indeed come as a shepherd for all. He himself said,

> I am the good *shepherd.* The good *shepherd* lays down his life for the sheep. John 10:11

Dr. Lapide proffers a most unique position and to some a very credible argument in purporting the purpose of the crucifixion. He states categorically that Jesus was a Jew and that He was crucified and resurrected. He sees the Easter morning event as the moment when non-Jewish believers entered into the spiritual family of the chosen people:

> Jesus was utterly true to the Torah, as I myself hope to be. I even suspect that Jesus was even more true to the Torah than I, an Orthodox Jew. I accept the resurrection of Easter Sunday not as an invention of the community of disciples, but as a historical event.... I believe that the Christ event leads to a way of salvation which God has opened up in order to bring the Gentile world into the community of God's Israel. Dr. Pinchas Lapide, Orthodox scholar

There is also this strong reference to the Savior of the Gentiles:

> Jesus was a Jew and a Jew he remained till his last breath. His one idea was to implant within his nation the idea of the coming of the Messiah and, by repentance and good works, hasten the 'end...' In all this, Jesus is the most Jewish of Jews... more Jewish than Hillel.... From the standpoint of general humanity, he is, indeed, 'a light

> to the Gentiles.'" Joseph Klausner, author and professor at Hebrew University

I was most surprised in researching material for this chapter to come across these lines written by my former Sunday School teacher. (I was not a regular Temple visitor)

> Jesus has become the most popular, the most studied, the most influential figure in the religious history of mankind.... No sensible Jew can be indifferent to the fact that a Jew should have had such a tremendous part in the religious education and direction of the human race.... Who can compute all that Jesus has meant to humanity? The love he has inspired, the solace he has given, the good he has engendered, the hope and joy he has kindled - all that is unequalled in human history.... The Jew cannot help glorying in what Jesus has meant to the world; nor can he help hoping that Jesus may yet serve as a bond between Jew and Christian, once his teaching is better known and the bane of misunderstanding at last is removed from his words and his ideal. Rabbi Hyman Enelow, past President of the Central Conference of American Rabbis

The greatest evidence of the validity and credibility of Jesus being the Messiah is the life changing spiritual process that has taken place in the life of millions of individuals and through every society through the centuries since Jesus walked on earth.

Jesus said:

> For the bread of God is he who comes down from heaven and gives life to the world... I am the bread

> of life. He who comes to me will never go hungry, and he who believes in me will never be thirsty.
>
> I am the living bread that came down from heaven. If anyone eats of this bread, he will live forever. This bread is my flesh, which I will give for the life of the world." John 6:50-51

*The Messiah's Fulfillment*

God revealed the meaning and purpose of sacrifice in history, especially through Moses in the Torah (Pentateuch). The collective teaching of the law *(Al-Sharia)* on the meaning of sacrifice as a ransom for sin is clear from the following words of Scripture:

> In fact, the law requires that nearly everything be cleansed with blood, and without the shedding of blood there is no forgiveness. Hebrews 9:22

Isaiah described the Messiah's sacrifice around 700 years before His coming:

> Surely he took up our infirmities and carried our sorrows, yet we considered him stricken by God, smitten by him, and afflicted. But he was pierced for our transgressions, he was crushed for our iniquities; the punishment that brought us peace was upon him, and by his wounds we are healed. We all, like sheep, have gone astray, each of us has turned to his own way; and the LORD has laid on him the iniquity of us all. He was oppressed and afflicted, yet he did not open his mouth; he was led like a lamb to the slaughter, and as a sheep

> before her shearers is silent, so he did not open his mouth.

He then began to teach them that,

> the Son of Man must suffer many things and be rejected by the elders, chief priests and teachers of the law, and that he must be killed and after three days rise again. Mark 8:31

Jesus predicts His death in Luke 18: 31,32

> Jesus took the Twelve aside and told them:
>
> We are going up to Jerusalem, and everything that is written by the prophets about the Son of Man will be fulfilled. He will be handed over to the Gentiles. They will mock him, insult him, spit on him, flog him and kill him. 33On the third day he will rise again.

The fulfillment of the promise is recorded in Matthew 26:53, 54

Jesus replied,

> Do you think I cannot call on my Father, and he will at once put at my disposal more than twelve legions of angels? But how then would the Scriptures be fulfilled that say it must happen in this way? Everything said will be accomplished.

*The Messiah's Promise- A Ransom for Many*

> The Messiah, who himself conquered death and raised the dead, says:
>
> > I am the resurrection and the life. He who believes in me will live, even though he dies; and whoever lives and believes in me will never die. John 11:25-26
>
> Yet to all who received him, to those who believed in his name, he gave the right to become children of God. John 1:12

I believe in the historical Jesus Christ, contained in our time, and that He was born of Mary, spent His life a servant of God, suffered and died willingly to atone for the sin of the world, and that He rose on the third day. He is the fulfillment of the Old Testament prophecies and filled the longing of my seeking heart for the Messiah, the Truth.

Christ's declaration that He was the awaited Messiah was not meant to provide great drama, though it is history's greatest drama. Christ did not come to enlighten us about values, though the world is the beneficiary of the highest ideology man will ever know.

Christ came as the Messiah to serve as the Lamb that was slain for your salvation and mine. The Messiah came, sent by God the Father, and He willingly died for the sins of the world. On the third day He was resurrected to proffer a hope for our re-birth, promising a more perfect path now and for eternity.

C.S. Lewis called Jesus, in his book, Surprised by Joy, "a transcendental interferer." I pray that the transcendental interferer has, through this book, helped you in your search for the Infinite. I hope that your seeking heart has been rewarded and that you too can acknowledge Him before men. If you do, His promise is,

"I will also acknowledge you before my Father in heaven."

## Chapter 17

### My soul has found a resting place

It is early summer, 2002, as I write these closing lines. Just a few months ago the reality was that the book might never have a last chapter.

On that January day my suitcase was packed and stood waiting at the front door. The following morning, in spite of the threat of a major snowstorm, I would be traveling three hours to New York City and check into a hospital for surgery. I had been in constant pain and incapacitated for the several months, confined to bed and the chair next to it. Months had been spent visiting the very best neurologists in the Northeast, seeking their therapeutic wisdom. They differed in prescribing treatment for my pain, yet all shared the consensus that surgery was the only real option.

Surgery can be unsettling at any age, more so when one is 88 years old. It is not that I feared the invasive procedure necessarily, but I knew that the recuperation would be long and discomforting. To be frank, I wished there was a pleasant option, one that would ensure a speedy return to the comfort of my home in Chester, Connecticut, and where I could go back to my active, daily routine, but there was none.

Between my bed and comfortable settee is a small table. My favorite books are arranged on the table in two piles, perhaps 14 or 16 in all, all of them religious in nature and all a private spiritual treasure trove. Most have been read several times and many are ear marked with passages significant to me. Those special pages are underlined or highlighted. In the pile are two books by a favorite author, Oswald Chambers. He writes in *Run Today's Race*, "Faith for my deliverance is not faith in God. Faith means, whether I am visibly delivered or not, I will stick to my belief that God is love. There are some things only learned in a fiery furnace." In the few days prior to departing for the hospital I shared with friends that my debilitating illness had brought me into a "fiery furnace".

I prayed Jesus' prayer in the Garden of Gethsemane and asked God to take "this cup from me." His answer? "Lo, I am with you always." God's answer is simple. He whispered the assurance in my ear that, "I am with you in your suffering and pain but it is more than compensated for in the love I shower on you. Evelyn, you are never alone." Jesus reminds us in the scriptures that "the kingdom of God is within you." My faith in all my tomorrows is grounded in my inner experience, God's faithfulness witnessed personally for almost a century.

It was in that assurance that I departed for Manhattan and the hospital, confident that God would guide the hands of the skilled surgeons, even as He soothed my spirit. As they attended to my physical repair and healing, God would sustain and continue to attend to my spiritual well being. He knew my every need. Although the outcome of the surgery would not be known for 24 hours, what was known then and forever is that God is love. I came to know and understand this ageless truth repeatedly during my life, for nearly 90 years. This truth began as a part of my healing during my four months at Blythewood. The period prior to Blythewood, however, was very different from today; I call it my "dark night of the soul". However,

I also realized that although I had found a solace within, I needed to face squarely the forces outside of me that had brought me to such despair in the first place. I no longer had the dark nights, but I knew that they would return if I did not seek a closer and deeper relationship with God. I knew too that there would be times when my spirit would be in the shadows. I also knew, that where the shadow is deepest, the Light is the brightest.

Joel Goldsmith wrote:

And so we go forward in what we think of as a quest, as a search. And as we do let us remember, we can know our progress by this: That every once in awhile, we see a horizon out there and we have the feeling, 'Oh, I've just a little a way to go and when I get this next point, I'll be there.' And so, we have that horizon as our goal. And you know it only takes a few days or weeks and all of a sudden, we come to that horizon and we see the whole world of spirit spread before us and we really believe we've entered the entire Kingdom of Heaven. And we have for a few days. And then all of a sudden we get used to this Light and we begin to notice just one more horizon over there that has to be traveled, 'just one more step and we'll be there.' But, I'm still finding horizons. That's one of the joys of this thing. I don't know what it would be like to ever get there and not find another horizon. I'm in no hurry to find out. I enjoy these horizons.

**My Life Is…**

**A never ending story,**
**Each time I reach my goal**
**New vistas rise before me**
**And beckon to my soul.**
**They challenge me to action**
**They tease and tantalize**
**With visions and new images**
**New truths to realize.**
**The call is irresistible**
**I can't evade or hide**
**I eagerly go forward**
**I'm tested and I'm tried**
**At last the victory**
**A lovely peace – and then**
**Once more the call**
**Break through that wall!**
**And off I go again.**

Evelyn Brill Stark

I had begun my exploration searching the horizon, my spiritual horizon as a child. In later years I began meditating daily, including reading the writings of spiritual mystics, praying, and simply waiting in silence for God to speak. They were my stepping-stones to a deeper faith. My faith became a belief – moving from faith in the verb form to faith as a noun. With time I recognized that I was moving upward, viewing new horizons, scanning new vistas, climbing a mountain of faith leading ever upward to the very heart of God.

Along the path He chose for me He carved out resting places. I needed time to reflect on what He was teaching me. He knew that I would need a place where I could abide to meditate on His love and goodness. Most often I spent those times of reflection on what appeared to be ledges in the mountainside. God granted me views created just for me beginning on a Maine hillside. Like that hillside, the expanse and the beauty He revealed were breathtaking. At times, however, I felt as though I was perched on a rocky ledge, afraid to move or to take another step. I realized then that I was in the shadow of the mountain. What had caused this?

As I thought back on those shadowy days, I realized that difficulties and worries had sought to overcome me, challenging my faith. The surgery planned for me was one of those shadowy moments. It was not that my faith faltered, simply the human worry that sometimes challenges the strongest spirit.

It was then that Selma's teaching and the precious promises of the 23rd Psalm came back to remind me that I was not alone in the shadows. My Shepherd was with me. The verses of the Psalm focus on God as the faithful and good Shepherd, and I was one of His flock. It tells us that He is the gracious host not only on the broad expanse but also is present and abides with us in the crevice.

As I climbed that mountain and basked at each resting place in God's glory I reflected on the many years of His faithfulness, not mine. I had known now, for many years, that I would never go back to the dark night of my soul. God had revealed Himself to me at Blythewood and He had brought me to ever-new heights in faith. He taught me not to fear the shadows in the crevices. I had come to realize that if there are shadows then there must also be Light. F.B. Meyer wrote, "God incarnate is the end of fear;

and the heart that realizes that He is in the midst... will be quiet in the middle of alarm." I learned how to be quiet and wait, even when in the shadow moments.

When I shared with a friend that I would soon be having surgery he asked if I was anxious; how strong is your faith? I replied, "The Lord is my shepherd, He comforts me. That has been my favorite Psalm since I was a child." He then shared a wonderful analogy of the 23rd Psalm words, where David speaks of "walking in the shadow," but without fear. He said, "The Psalm has been called the Nightingale Psalm. The hauntingly beautiful song of the Nightingale is sung long before the sun rises, sung in assurance as a welcome to the dawn. While the night is still full and dark the Nightingale sings its song of hope and of faith, it sings knowing from millenniums of sweet singing that even though it be dark the light will come."

Even though we may be in the shadow we can take to heart the assurance that He who created light is in us. He is with us in all things even as we wait for the light. I knew that God would journey with me to the hospital and that His love would surround me through that trying experience. My writing these last pages is testimony to His loving care. He brought me through, and it is His desire that I honor my Shepherd's care through the completion of this book.

The surgeons told me that the operation had gone well. They added, however, "due your age and the delicate procedures you have undergone you will require a lengthy recovery period." I had been warned to expect pain and discomfort for "perhaps several months." They provided me prescriptions drugs of various sorts. Some were anti-infection remedies and others pain killers. They also recommended that I use a wheel chair until such time that I be strong enough to use a walker. I listened attentively to the doctor's advice. After a final consultation I was wheeled to the elevator where we said our farewells.

On my return home from the hospital I pondered what was next for me. I prayed to my Shepherd asking that He reveal His agenda for me. I reflected on words I penned some years ago, seeking His direction,

**Waiting**

**I'm waiting to hear**
**I'm waiting to know**
**What you want me to do**
**Where you want me to go.**

**Beholding the wonder**
**The joy of your ways**
**Each hour brings blessings**
**That hallow my days**

**My heart overflows**
**With your peace and your grace**
**I will share it in prayer**
**With the whole human race.**

I had been away from home for almost a week and a pile of letters were waiting my response. None were get-well cards because I had decided not to share the scheduled surgery with but a few close friends. The correspondence waiting replies were from my "spiritual" family, friends from around the world. The letters were from friends newly made, and others from persons I had known through correspondence for decades. There were also Emails from *NEW VISION* magazine (formerly *Science of Thought Review*) advising me that they were going to publish a trilogy that I had submitted some weeks before. They needed some biographical input and information on my earlier book. There were also invitations to visit various book clubs and retirement homes requesting that I come and recite my poems. I was very active doing so until the autumn of 2001 when my health failed me

I prayed, "God please give me the healing and strength necessary to continue to share **The joy of your ways.**

Do I really need to tell you the answer to that prayer?

God's answer was extraordinary! Within two days of coming home, I was on my feet. The wheel chair remained in a warehouse and hundreds of pills were thrown out! The pain I had been warned about never came. I knew immediately that God had healed me. It was clear He had future plans for me to be fruitful in His service. My recuperation belied all of the specialist's experience.

Joel's request to his devotees was, *'Carry on.'* Katherine Glover shared with us his desire that *"the work would go on in every direction, with increased momentum. The most important thing each of us can do is to express, to teach what we have received."*

My insight, long inspired and directed by Joel, has grown steadily since his passing forty years ago. It has taken me beyond the unfolding illumination experienced during my twelve years with him. I have learned to fully abide in the Spirit and to let the Spirit abide in me.

Looking back over these last four decades since Joel passed on I humbly share John's words in his 15th chapter that the Spirit "Has made every provision for our fruitfulness... I appointed you to go on and bear fruit, fruit that shall last; so that the Father may give you all that you ask in my name." I take that precious promise to my heart asking the Father to take my written words and consecrate them in His service.

The question I am often asked is what must I do to be saved, to have the Spirit in me? The scriptures tell us we will be judged according to what has been revealed to us by the Spirit, by our knowledge, and our conscious acceptance of His revelations.

I believe the earnestness of our seeking will determine where we spend eternity. Our spirit determines how and what we seek, what we allow to enter our soul.

**Inwardly I Sing**

**Sweet harmony of life**
**Enfold me.**
**Thy perfect peace will bring release**
**To soothe my heart**
**Dispelling all the pain and sadness. Thou art the Way.**
**I trust in thee to set me free – eternally.**

**How tenderly thy peace**
**Enfolds me.**
**In thy embrace I feel thy grace**
**It fills my heart**
**Dissolving all the pain and sadness. How blessedly**
**I rest in thee – my spirit free.**

Evelyn Brill Stark

The purpose of this book, my message, is that all who seek God will be free to share the spirit of the Infinite. It is an inner longing and release to the Divine, acknowledging who you truly are.

**When You Know Who You Are**

**When you know who you are you are free.**
**There is no longer the little "i"**
**To be hurt or angry or anything negative. You are Love.**
**You have compassion for those who do not know**
**They are Love, too,**
**But are trapped in their ego beliefs.**
**You try to help them know who they are**
**So they can be free, too.**
**So they can know they are Love.**

Evelyn Brill Stark

Joel wrote, "You can never succeed because God is the only activity, but you can be the instrument for God's work. You can be the instrument for God's labor; you can be the instrument for God's love…."

That is the pathway to, and of the Infinite Way. I pray it may be so…

## Epilogue

**Moment by moment I'm kept in His love...**

It was the day before Mother's Day, May 2002. I was visiting a friend in Manhattan who lives near Central Park, a place of many wonderful memories. I had ice-skated on many of its ponds as a child with Selma along to keep an eye on me. Morty and I had strolled through the park celebrating our engagement. It was the place of solace during my recuperation following my Blythewood stay. And I would often wander the meandering paths arm in arm with Morty en route to a luncheon at the Plaza or the New York Athletic Club.

It was a wonderful spring day and my friend and I walked aimlessly, without many words to each other. We found a bench next to a pond, in fact the exact same location where I had sat countless times through my almost ninety years. I was basking in nostalgia when my friend informed me that she had many errands to run. I told her I preferred to stay in the park a bit longer and that I would join her later in the day. We waved each other goodbye and off she went. I remained in the park for another half hour or so before setting off to my friend's apartment.

I exited Central Park at Fifth Avenue and 63rd Street. The slight breeze reminded me that the Central Park Zoo was nearby. I noticed that the small area separating the sidewalk from the streets was cobble stoned. I was very careful as I stepped gingerly across the bumpy stones. I struggled to maintain my balance, but to no avail. With arms flailing I fell with a great thud… Taxis, limos and cars sped by, slowing ever slightly to see why a crowd had quickly formed near the sidewalk. I lay absolutely still waiting for my body to signal to my brain where and how badly I was injured. Then the strangest thing happened.

As I lay prostrate on the ground a young face suddenly appeared next to mine, only inches away. I had not yet picked my head up from the stones. I saw dozens of feet behind her head as she said, "I am here for you… I will stay with you… I will not leave you…" "Who are you", I asked. She replied, "My name is Nathalie". She spoke with an accent and I asked, "Where are you from?" She replied, "Venezuela."

Someone, possibly the policeman in the crowd, had telephoned for an ambulance and I could hear the siren's wail nearing me. Nathalie stayed with me, holding my hand, and entered the ambulance for the ride to Roosevelt Hospital. She remained at my side as the emergency room doctors examined and evaluated my condition. In fact the only time she left me was when she departed my room in order to break a date with her boyfriend later that evening. True to her word, that "angel of mercy" remained until my discharge several hours later.

As I lay motionless on that 5th Avenue sidewalk the thought came naturally, "Why me and why now!" Couldn't the Infinite see fit to just let me live out whatever few months or years I have left in peace and solitude? All I had wanted was to enjoy a little private time in the park where so much of my healing had taken place – where the Infinite and I had become one.

The following day I telephoned Nathalie. She had insisted I do so as she was anxious to know how I was progressing. The first thing she said was, "Happy Mother's Day!" She went on to exude how very happy she was that I was feeling better (good thing she didn't see my face and side – black, blue, and green) and told me a bit about her self.

Nathalie, 26 years old, had come to New York seven months earlier, leaving her mother and several siblings in Venezuela. She had been unable to find work and was living in a small studio apartment in Queens. Money was running out and she could no longer afford to make her weekly calls to her mother wherein she would wind a convincing tale that all was well. The last few days, those heralding the approach of Mother's Day, had been particularly difficult as Nathalie realized how extremely homesick and lonely she was. She told me she was taking pills to overcome her depression and despondency, although she wouldn't tell me what kind of pills.

She shared with me that it was her intent to commit suicide and that she was in Central Park plotting the next step as she walked along the park's entrance, pills in hand. It was at that time that she saw me fall. Then came the most extraordinary statement. "Mrs. Stark, you gave me a reason to live! I really feel that God placed you in my path and that it was He that brought you into my life. He wanted me to come to your side, to comfort you and to give you strength through my remaining with you. In some mysterious way I felt your pain in me!" I pondered for a moment and replied, "Nathalie, what I am going to say to you may sound very strange, but… when I fell I hurt physically beyond words. But when you took hold of my hand I sensed a very special love, a love not of this world.

My suffering left me and was passed to you and your youthful body because you could handle what I couldn't. But at the same time I felt that your emotional pain was transferred to me – to me because I knew from experience that I could give it over to God…"

We spoke for a few minutes more before saying good-bye and promising to stay in touch. I thought to myself how ironic the drama of those two days. In that same park where God had healed and restored my faith a half century earlier, I was now the vessel He used in giving a sense of self worth and value to a young lady. She was experiencing abandonment and loneliness in the midst of teeming hoards just as I had. At the very same moment God used her as an instrument to relieve my physical pain.

In John 13: 33 Jesus says to His disciples,

"*Little children*, I am with you a little while longer. You will seek Me; and as I said to the Jews, now I also say to you, 'Where I am going, you cannot come.' A new commandment I give to you, that you love one another, even as I have loved you, that you also love one another. By this all men will know that you are My disciples, if you have love for one another."

Those who Jesus called to His side and service had spent years at His side, walking, sleeping, talking, laughing, and weeping. They watched Him perform miracles. Some saw Him die and be resurrected. Yet, He called them His *little children.* One could perhaps see the remark as a rebuke, for their not having understood earlier who He was and His mission. But to my mind it was the most endearing title possible Jesus loved the disciples in their simplicity and naivety

Key in Jesus' admonition is to realize that all who claim Him as Messiah stand side by side with the disciples in having to obey Jesus' words.

I suppose all readers would wish that Jesus had cut the commandment short and left it at "Love one another!" After all, one could interpret Jesus' words as having to then be applied in human terms; love as much as you can. But He didn't leave it there. "Love as I love" requires an understanding of pain, a willingness to suffer and allow the experience of abandonment and betrayal to become personal. It demands that we have what Paul called "This mind in you", the mind of Christ.

In Isaiah God says: "I am the Lord, I have called you in righteousness, I have taken you by the hand and kept you." What a powerful, ageless assurance that is in the times of turmoil and suffering that beset us all. But to say that God keeps us is to tell only half of the story and to read only half of the verse. For it goes on to say: "I have given you as a covenant to the people, a light to the nations." Which we can translate as: I command you to witness to the difference God's love has brought to your life.

700 years later a proud father, God, expressed the duality of keeping and giving clearly in Jesus' baptism. When Jesus comes up out of the water, God's hand reaches down and holds onto him. The Spirit of God alights on Jesus and He says, "This is my Son, the Beloved, with whom I am well pleased." (Luke 3;22) The words of God translate as, "I intend to keep him…to hold onto him and never let him go!"

And yet, in the same moment God also gives Jesus to a needy world, to heal where there is sickness, to challenge where there is complacency, to bring peace where there is strife, to invite where there is exclusion, to bring light where there is darkness. In the very same way, God holds me, while also giving me back to the world to touch the world as on Jesus' behalf.

"Love one another as I love you…" The imperative is not love one another, but love one another as I love. What a difference those three words make; *as I love*! Human love versus God's love…

"The Lord your God test you…"
Deut. 13:3

One of the most wonderful manifestations of the Christian life is to be tied into God's purpose and plan not only for this time on earth but for eternity. As I reflect back on the last few months I must admit that, with the writing of this book completed, I saw little purpose for God not taking me home to be with Morty. But God tested my devotion.

Everything, which concerns the Kingdom, must be proved before God. All along the pilgrimage we are being tested as by fire, a fire that purifies both our character and service. God looks at our character not ever on outward appearances as He works through His "children" for eternity. The progress of my spiritual growth would have been hampered had it been my initiative or design. But the scriptures tell us that He who has begun a good work in us will work patiently to perfect it. Perfect it He will until I stand before Him in eternity.

We have a wonderful promise found in John 15, "Abide in me and I in you. He that abides in me, and I in him, he it is that bears much fruit. It is the fruit of faith and not dependent on my own moral striving. The beauty of that truth is that we need not rely on our own limited strength and resources, God almighty promises to control and direct us. A metaphor from Mahayana Buddhism illustrates well, we are not like the infant monkey seeking to avoid falling by clinging with every ounce of strength to its mother; we are instead, like the kitten, carried gently from place to place in its mother's mouth.

Christ has given us hope. He understands us--our temptations, our discouragements, our concerns about tomorrow. His abiding love helps us in every facet of this life and assures hope for the life to come.

**What God Hath Promised**

**God hath not promised**
**Skies always blue,**
**Flower-strewn pathways**
**All our lives through;**
**God hath not promised**
**Sun without rain,**
**Joy without sorrow,**
**Peace without pain.**
**But God hath promised**
**Strength for the day,**
**Rest for the labor,**
**Light for the way,**
**Grace for the trials,**
**Help from above,**
**Unfailing sympathy,**
**Undying love.**

Annie Johnson Flint

II.

My recuperation was speedy and relatively without much pain. Doctors and friends were all amazed at how quickly I was back to my old self, or should I say my youthful self. Joel Goldsmith wrote, "Healing is finding an inner communion with something greater, far greater, than anything in the world.... The body, then, begins to show forth perfect, complete health, youth, vitality, and strength, all the gift from the Lord."

Do I dare say that my body showed "youth" at 88! Many who visited me on my return home shared exactly those words. Most had visited me only weeks earlier when I also experienced almost immediate recovery following my back surgery. The walk to my little apartment from the reception area takes 4 or 5 minutes and then a short elevator ride followed by a walk down an embankment to my door. Within days of my return, my face still discolored from the fall, I walked without any difficulty to the elevator where I would greet my many visitors. Without exception, all were amazed that I could walk without the aid of a cane the doctors insisted I would need. In fact, more than once I did a little dance to show just how agile and energetic I was!

Spring had come to New England in all its glory! Much time was spent relaxing, reading, writing to friends, and doing a final edit of the book. As the days passed I watched as trees began to bud and bushes sprang to life. Spring flowers sprouted new life with every intermittent shower. As spring brought new life to the earth I basked in the knowledge that I too was experiencing a rebirth, a physical healing. I knew too though, that my joy was complete because of the spiritual healing that was so much a part of my consciousness. My spiritual dimension lifted me from any thoughts of physical hurt or psychological depression.

I must add that I was not alone in seeking physical healing for myself. Friends both near and far had somehow sensed that I had been injured. Several wrote to me directly and others through friends asking. “Is everything all right with Evelyn?” One friend, from England, sent an Email showing concern stating, “I sense Evelyn is in great pain, tell her our prayer group is lifting her to the Eternal.” I was pleased to write back and share that “your prayers were answered even before God heard them.”

In the weeks following I researched several publishers recommended to me, both here and abroad, those I felt could provide the best possible distribution network for my book – God's message through me. I was also busy editing the book. One avenue of marketing unheard of a few years ago but today a must is the World Wide Web, and a website for this book was designed. I had seen a print-out of the web site and was anxious to see it on a computer monitor. The closest place where I could do this was my local library in Chester Village. I scheduled a visit and looked forward to seeing it!

My friend who was driving me there called for me and we walked the long walkway from my apartment to the front entrance of my building when I suddenly stumbled and found myself flat on the floor. I knew immediately that I had broken my arm and perhaps even worse. The pain was more than I could bear – I lay motionless hoping the pain would subside, but it didn't. An ambulance was called and I was rushed to the emergency room in the largest hospital in my area, a journey of some 20 minutes. Several x-rays were taken and it was determined that I had experienced a compacted fracture of the upper arm and a dislocated shoulder. The doctors tried to reset my shoulder through manual manipulation several times albeit without success. It was decided that surgery was the only option and that an artificial rotator cup would be implanted. The surgery was performed the next day. My face was black and blue, my knees injured and my lower back in pain.

In the space of 24 hours I had gone from a state of spiritual bliss and physical well being to absolute torment. Why would the Infinite inflict such pain on me… three traumatic hospital experiences in the space of 4 months!

Due my extreme pain the doctors advised the hospital staff to put me in a private room. They knew from experience that there would be occasions during the night when I would cry out in pain. They were anxious that I not disturb other patients. To my great surprise, following the surgery and one night's rest, I was moved to a different room, a room I had to share with another patient. I was resentful that this was done without my knowledge or approval. I let the hospital staff know of my displeasure but their sympathetic reply was simply, "we are as sorry as you are." I could not understand the reason for the change in rooms, but God would soon show me.

I asked the nurse about the ailments of my roommate and was told, "She is worse off than you are!" I thought to myself, "then she must be in absolute misery…" The curtain dividing the room was not drawn so I had the opportunity to view the patient in the next bed. She was a large African American woman who appeared to be comatose. I was told her name was Mrs. Cora Turner. There was no response from her as I introduced myself. I silently prayed for God's blessings and mercy on her.

I was given intravenous drugs in addition to orally administered painkillers. They provided a modicum of relief and also helped me fall asleep. I awoke intermittently through the afternoon, and again some hours later to find the entire room filled to overflowing with friends of Mrs. Turner. All the chairs in the room were occupied and the entourage lined the walls and flowed into the hallway. People of different ages were coming and going throughout the afternoon and early evening. I thought to myself that Mrs. Turner must be very loved to have so many visitors wishing her well.

As I opened my eyes I noticed that many were weeping and that every tearful eye was focused on me, studying me as though I was on parade. I said, "Good evening. How wonderful it must be for Mrs. Turner to have so many loving friends to visit her bedside." The reply came from more than one person, "We are more than friends; we are family. That's our aunt Cora!" I learned later that even those who were not directly related called her Aunt Cory.

I was pleased to share with them that I had prayed for Cory immediately on entering the room some hours earlier. I explained that I had a private room but for some inexplicable reason I had been forced to move. I went on to share that I understood now that I was sent there by the Eternal to comfort Cory. The room very quickly became a sanctuary… All of us sensed God's presence; we were one in spirit, one with God.

While we spoke a man entered the room wearing a clerical collar and a gold cross suspended from a chain on his chest. He was very thin and frail. He walked to Cory's bed and bent over her speaking to no one. I prayed silently that he might bring comfort to Cory and all in the room. I opened my eyes to look around the room to find that all in the room had their eyes closed and heads bowed in prayer.

Prior to the Minister's departure he came to my bed and leaned over and whispered, "God bless you. You have brought a very special sense of peace to this room – when I visited these people yesterday, they were distraught, fearful for the future. Today they are at peace." As the Minister left the room he said, "Look at you all – when I arrived you cried. Now that I'm leaving you all smile!"

We all laughed together realizing that God's love filled the room.

I prayed silently thanking God that He who held me close to Him had also sent me to these, His children needing comfort. How wonderful to know that He placed me just where I was most needed.

Joel told me, "Illumination first brings peace, then confidence and assurance; it brings rest from the world's contests, and then all good flows to us through Grace." Illumination had brought me peace and also the confidence to share His grace.

The hospital staff came shortly after the Minister departed and wheeled Aunt Cory out of the room. I was told that she had not opened her eyes or spoken in many days and that she was being taken to the Intensive Care Unit. She had apparently been unconscious for the last several days. I said to the many friends of Aunt Cory, "Live the moment – rejoice in these times you share with her. I'm certain she knows you are here. Live the moment and watch the future unfold…" Myrtle, one of the visitors thanked me for my words. She said, "Thank you Evelyn for being in this room." I replied, "God placed me here…"

Then they left the room one by one wishing me well.

The following afternoon my dismissal papers were being filled out and my bag was packed for the trip back home, when to my surprise Aunt Cory was wheeled back into the room, but this time in a wheel chair, not a gurney. More surprising than that was when she opened her mouth and spoke to me! Less than 24 hours earlier she had been brought to the ICU because she had" taken a turn for the worse." I do not know who coined that phrase but to my mind it must certainly have been someone uncertain of where his next step would take him. I shared this thought with Aunt Cory and she replied, "My Lord must have some reason for keeping me… to keep me from His side – which in my view would have been a turn for the best!" We both laughed… I said to her, "Our Lord both holds us and sends us out. I'm so pleased that He sent me to you. This room was like a cathedral yesterday as your friends, family, Minister, and I prayed here. I have visited some of the great cathedrals both here in the U.S.A. and abroad, but none was ever more tenderly blessed than this one."

I regret I don't recall the author's name, and perhaps that's what he would wish, but his words are a tribute that I pray I can take for myself.

> "He built no great cathedral, that centuries applaud.
> But in his daily living, his life cathedraled God."

May my life be a living temple in which the Infinite resides and from which His blessings flow….

Evelyn Brill Stark, August, 2002.

## Index of Poems

*by Evelyn Brill Stark*

I dedicate this book to the people whose lives have influenced and transformed my living from finite to infinite as I have searched and found the real meaning of life. Without their love and support throughout my life this book would not have been possible.

| | |
|---|---|
| My Beloved Husband | Morty |
| My Teacher | Joel |
| My Doctor | Vessie |
| My Father | Henry Brill |
| My Spiritual Mother | Selma |
| My Friend | Lorry |

*I must also express my heartfelt appreciation to Sven who is not only my co-author, but also now a friend.*

Evelyn Brill Stark

# Evelyn Brill Stark, Chester, Ct. 2002

Portrait by Judy Perry, Old Saybrook, Ct.